— THE —

PRICING
ROADMAP

How to Design B2B SaaS Pricing Models
That Your Customers Will Love

— THE —

PRICING
ROADMAP

ULRIK LEHRSKOV-SCHMIDT

HOUNDSTOOTH
PRESS

THE PRICING ROADMAP

How to Design B2B SaaS Pricing Models That Your Customers Will Love

ISBN	978-1-5445-3630-9	*Hardcover*
	978-1-5445-3631-6	*Paperback*
	978-1-5445-3632-3	*Ebook*

To my sons, Adam and Amos.
I'm proud of you.

CONTENTS

PREFACE

Here is a piece of advice: "Never talk about a book you haven't finished writing yet." I started working with pricing almost by chance in 2017, after writing a book on pricing psychology (available only in Danish) together with my wife and partner in almost anything, Sally Khallash.

In 2018, I started to focus specifically on business-to-business software-as-a-service (B2B SaaS) pricing, and I got so much business it was hard to keep up. Many of the world's largest venture and private equity firms referred their portfolio companies to me, and I even became the preferred pricing partner of the Microsoft Western Europe's independent software vendors (ISV) program. Why? I had a key insight that resonated: pricing is more a "design" job than an "Excel" job.

Then, in early 2020, I announced I was going to write this book. I had a few customers and newsletter subscribers, like Maarten Laurel, who kept checking in with me and asking, "How is the book doing?" Without their support and constant prompting, I would never have finished this.

I am indebted to all those customers in 2018–2020 who allowed me to test ideas and use their businesses to create the frameworks and insights that form the core of this book. It wasn't always pretty.

I have also been blessed with a lot of customers who are happy to share their stories. That is brave, and I'm grateful to be able to use their cases as test cases, examples, frameworks, and so forth. I apologize in advance for the misrepresentations that are bound to happen when writing them up.

--- ONE ---

WHY PRICING IS HARD

YOU ARE ASKING THE WRONG QUESTION

I talk to about a hundred B2B SaaS executives and entrepreneurs every year.

All of them are brilliant people who work incredibly hard. Many—especially the entrepreneurs—have created amazing innovations that sometimes are just so mind-bogglingly brilliant that I have to constantly revise my expectation of what the future will look like. Because if we can make "that"...then there seems to be no limitations to where we can take "this" as a society.

Some of these people—especially the big corporate product teams and executives—are just so incredibly detail oriented. They have poured hundreds of hours into answering the tiniest questions about their customers and back up their decisions with massive organizational power. I find it truly awe inspiring what kind of change happens in the world when a billion-dollar enterprise really decides to kick the ball and move something.

All of them are extremely focused on their customers and bringing value to them through their products. Obviously. Because if you don't do that, you are not even in the game.

And yet, when it comes to pricing, everyone seems confused.

When we create a great product that brings some value into the world, we go and ask our customers what they are willing to pay for that—or we simply stick a price on it, ask them to pay, and then see what happens.

Usually what happens is this: some customers will buy and some won't. Okay, so far, so good—at least now you're in business.

But the customers who don't buy will tell you that you are out of your mind with your pricing—and that if you only lowered it, they would become customers. Okay, that's great. Except that to get these customers on board you'll have to lower prices for everyone. Right? And then your average revenue per customer (ARPU is the shorthand we often use)[1] will drop.

While "more customers × less money" might be a good idea, it is not necessarily so. You may suspect that some customers who actually do buy your product might be willing to pay quite a lot more.

I once helped a €100M insurtech SaaS business fix their pricing model after they had just landed a €1M annual contract with an insurance company. They were thrilled because they had been chasing this customer for years...until they realized that during the two months of scoping and conversations with the insurance company's business managers and procurement department, they had not negotiated the price even a single time! Not once. They had simply accepted the €1M annual recurring price (which even came with a three-year tie-in period) at face value.

They later found out through back channels that the insurance company was staring down an imminent €30M IT development

---

1 ARPU is generally a business-to-consumer (B2C) concept, but it's so central to the commercial value of a product that it is used throughout this book, despite our focus on B2B.

project—with an estimated €5M annual internal maintenance cost—to build something that could only deliver perhaps 20 percent of what my client's product could.

Ouch![2]

So pricing often seems like a catch-22: if you raise prices, you lose customers but gain more from the ones who stay on. If you lower prices, you gain more customers but lose out on the money (and margin) you make on each one.

I've seen this question—let's call it "the Price Optimization Problem"—drive SaaS executives to the brink of insanity. Some even spend years and years trying to figure out how to even begin to answer this question.

But they can't.

Because asking yourself, "What should my product or service cost?" is the wrong question.

Let me explain using the "killer app" of the 1860s as a case story: trains!

Figure 1: The "Killer App" of the 1860s: A Steam Train.
Source: Otho Moore's 1912 photo of Fast Passenger Engine 3033 in the Indio Southern Pacific yards. Circa 1912.

---

2 Luckily, we found out this misrepresentation was systemic, so we managed to raise prices by around 60% with no churn.

SAAS IS LIKE A TRAIN: IT COSTS A FORTUNE TO BUILD BUT NOTHING TO RUN

In the 1800s, steam power went from being a niche interest of curious British aristocrats to being the core fuel of the Industrial Revolution, changing the world at a breakneck phase.

The world's first inter-city passenger railroad line sprung up between Manchester and Liverpool in 1830, and it was soon obvious to anyone and everyone that railroads would be the key factor between which countries made it and which didn't. (Just like software today.) They lowered the cost of transportation and labor to a point that seemed to be so close to zero that it was just unbelievable. (Just like software today.)

The US jumped on that wagon big time. Railroad companies shot up on both the east and west coasts—often with federal or state backing—and started connecting all the big cities, but no one had yet linked east to west. People still had to walk all the way across the continent from the overpopulated, dirty cities of the east to the promised frontier in the west, where land was cheap (or even free).

This journey would easily take six months and several thousand dollars—in 1860s money![3]—and many would die. From the cold in the Appalachian Mountains. From disease outbreaks in the caravans. From starvation. From attacks by Native Americans (who understandably weren't too keen on this new venture).

So the price to move from east to west for the average 1860s American was basically *all* of their money, six months of strenuous marching, and perhaps their life! And the chance that you'd ever be able to go back to visit friends and family on the east coast?

---

3 In the 1860s, $7,000 would be the equivalent of around a quarter of a million now.

Zero. When you made that decision, that was it. You were gone. The west might as well have been a different planet. This was a one-way ticket to Mars.

So the migration from east to west was too slow.

To the railroad companies, that was their "use case."

They knew that by building a "transcontinental railroad," they could bring the price for a one-way ticket from Philadelphia in the east to Sacramento in the west down to about $6.[4]

But just like with developing software, you don't make any money building railroads until you actually solve that use case. It's all planning and building—for years!—before you get to open the doors and invite customers in and take their money. But—again, just like with software—once you actually do open the doors, the unit economics of the individual customers are quite good.

In accounting speak, we might say: "big capital investments in building the product but low operational costs in running the business once it's in the market."

This is the pitch 100 percent of entrepreneurs make to VCs when pitching their business: scale! "We need all this money *now* to build this great product. But once we've built it, it will sell like hotcakes, and nearly all that revenue will be pure profit because delivery and production costs are either zero or near zero."

But hidden within this great promise of the perfect unit economic of 100 percent pure, unadulterated delicious profit also lies a pricing problem: if it costs us basically zero to take a passenger across the continent—and their alternative is several thousand dollars plus the risk of death—then what should the ticket cost?

Software (and trains!) are different from many physical product

4 Around $200 today; that's more like it!

companies in this way: because their unit costs are (near) zero, they can't really create pricing from a simple markup on their unit costs.

If it costs Starbucks 10¢ to make a cup of coffee plus another 85¢ in barista salaries and rent, then charging $1.90 for that cup of coffee is simply a 100 percent markup. In other words, they just double the unit's cost base, which leaves 95¢ in gross profit to pay for general advertising, back-office administration, stock options, taxes, and all the rest. That is how literally 90 percent of businesses do pricing.

But that doesn't work for SaaS companies, who face a whole host of pricing complexities that the likes of Starbucks don't have to worry about. Let's take a look at those complexities in more detail.

YOU WILL NEVER HEAR THAT YOUR PRICES ARE TOO LOW

This is the siren song of SaaS pricing (and transcontinental railroads): once it's made, you'll make a profit on any individual sale—regardless of price!

Let's say that you have a varied market for your new transcontinental railroad, like these guys:

Figure 2: Three Classes of Potential Railroad Customers.
Source: Library of Congress Prints and Photographs Division, Washington, LC-USZ62-118006.

One rich. One poor. One in-between.

Obviously, they can (and might be willing to) pay different amounts for the ticket to California.

Following the question implicit in the Optimization Problem ("What should my product cost?"), you end up with a price something like this:

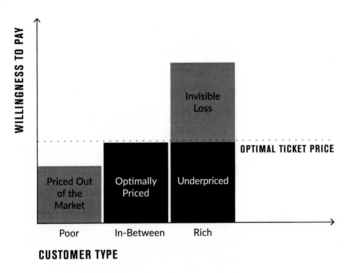

Figure 3: Price optimization balances lost customers with loss on customers willing to pay more.

By optimizing the price of your ticket, you end up with the maximum price your in-between customers will pay. The rich customers will also pay—happily! They get a better deal than they would have been willing to agree to, and you lose out on charging them more.

And, crucially, they are unlikely to tell you. Or rather, they will tell you all that's wrong with your product: "We really like this idea of transporting people to California really cheaply, but how about adding, perhaps, some end-to-end encryption, advanced roles and permissions, and maybe a single-sign-on?" You know the type.

Also, you will have a long tail of "poor" customers who find your train just too expensive. If they are really nice to you, they will actually tell you. And if they are really, *really* nice to you, then they will tell you in no uncertain terms how insanely overpriced and unaffordable your solution is. How you've totally sold out, gone insane, forgotten where you came from, have become greedy, and all the other loving, carefully crafted feedback great potential customers will provide (for free!).

So this is the Optimization Problem: no matter where you price yourself in your market of potential customers, each "end" of that market seems to scream its own specific kind of feedback at you—and all of this perfectly reasonable customer feedback can really paralyze a SaaS team. Because how do you make a decision about pricing when you're getting such varied feedback from across your market?

Of course, your product *should* be better. Right? And since the unit cost is zero, why not sell to the poor and claim that profit? At least until you break even and your MRR can pay for your overhead. And then—when you cross that sweet "profit horizon"—every sale is not only pure gross profit but pure actual, hard, bottom-line, put-in-the-bank, shareholder-friendly net profit.

And then, *then*, you can raise prices!

Pricing for the poor and building products for the rich is the wrong solution, but it's also the solution I see 90 percent of SaaS companies go for. Especially the venture-backed ones, although even corporates can fall for this as well.

Yes, it is true that a "land-and-expand" strategy, where you first focus on customer volume before you focus on customer profit, can work for some SaaS companies. But unless you can check a very specific set of boxes, you are not one of those companies.

Even if you are, it's a strategy that kills more companies than it saves. Far more. Yes, you too.

A land-and-expand strategy is incredibly hard to execute, and it requires boatloads of suicidal capital and more than a little luck. The only thing it has going for it is that it saves you from actually thinking too hard about your pricing and making, you know, real, might-fail, skin-in-the-game decisions.

So here is the deal: read this book. If you still want to give your product away to enable future profit, then more power to you. But at least determine if you have a real alternative first.

Now, let's take a look at what that alternative might be.

THE MONEY IS IN THE PRICING STRUCTURE— NOT THE PRICE POINT

THE RIGHT UNIT OF ANALYSIS

The alternative is to ask a different question. When you are asking, "How should I price my product or service?" your core unit of analysis is your own product. It's what you deliver to the market.

The reason it is impossible (not hard, impossible!) to put a price tag on that is because it's not what your customer is buying! Your customer is trying to get something done. And that "something" isn't the same for all customers. In fact, it's not even remotely the same.

Instead of trying to price your product, you should price your customer.

Your product is the wrong unit of analysis. It will always lead you down a rabbit hole of conflicting feedback from the market. The "invisible loss" on the "rich" customers will always be in direct opposition to the "visible loss" of the "poor" customers. Lowering one will always increase the other.

The solution is to charge different prices for different customers. You know, first-class vs. second-class vs. third-class tickets.

The train companies instantly realized: to maximize revenue on the transcontinental railroad, they would have to differentiate the value propositions to different customer classes. They would charge them what they were willing to pay—introducing the killer features of the dining wagon and fancy accommodation.

Regardless of which ticket you bought, you would still be getting the same overall result: going to California. With a first-class ticket, however, you would travel there in style. For some passengers (not all, crucially), that is important and something they are willing to pay lots of money for.

THE THIRD-CLASS PROBLEM

Introducing the luxury option of traveling in first class solved the problem of properly monetizing the more affluent passengers.

However, a lot of people moving west were poor European immigrants who had staked their entire lives' savings on this journey in order to establish a better life. They had already crossed the Atlantic Ocean, and a six-day train ride to go west wasn't really seen as an opportunity for luxury.

So while they had the money to spend on a second-class ticket, they were just not willing to pay extra for comfort. They would much rather spend what little money they had in California once they got there. They would buy the third-class tickets instead.

Because those tickets would sell out quickly, leaving empty seats in the second class, the railroad companies—just like any good product team—would try and tweak their value offerings. They would remove features like "chairs" and "clean" from the third-class wagons, even going so far as to introduce old cattle wagons as the third-class option, still with manure and all.

But the immigrants remained frugal. As long as they would get to California, it didn't really matter how, and the money stayed in their pockets.

So what to do? How do you differentiate between second- and third-class tickets to properly prompt your customers to buy the options you know they can afford?

If you've ever created a freemium option for a piece of software and had a hard time getting your users to upgrade to the first paid tier, then you can appreciate the problem that was facing the railroad tycoons with the third-class tickets.

The solution?

Take the roofs off the wagons.

Figure 4: Transcontinental Train with Roof Removed.
Source: Andrew J. Russell / Yale Collection of Western Americana, Beinecke Rare Book and Manuscript Library

The railroad actually solves two problems instead of one, and if you're a cold-hearted, capitalist railroad tycoon, then you might realize that the solutions your product solves can be separated:

1. You get to California.

2. Without dying.

The cold in the Appalachian Mountains can kill you—whether you walk across or ride the train—so the railroad reintroduced the feature of "death" to the third-class passengers by removing the roofs from the wagons. The pricing question for passengers then became: "Do I want to risk not getting to California because I'm too cheap to buy a ticket that will get me there alive?"

Suffice to say that the open wagons were a staple of third-class tickets for years. And the railroad companies made an absolute killing.

The problem for many software companies (and maybe even for the cold-hearted railroad tycoons, who knows) is that nobody builds a product to kill people who use it.

In fact, if you've bothered to spend the time and capital to build the damn thing, then I bet you'd actually like all your passengers to receive a truly first-class experience!

Don't price the railroad. Or even the number of miles traveled (although you should probably do that also). First, think of pricing your customer.

So pull the roof off your software. Determine what discreet, small problems you solve that you take for granted, feature by feature. Then look at your customers and try to decide what they are actually willing to pay for. Which features are really optional when it comes down to it? Like surviving.

So 99 percent of all SaaS businesses get pricing wrong because they are trying to "find the right price for their product," when what they should be doing is looking at their potential customer base and asking, "How do I build a pricing structure that will properly price all these customers?"

If you and your team are debating $119 vs. $149, you've already lost. The money is not in the price point. It's in the price structure.

Don't price your product. Price your customer.

THE PRICING DESIGN PROCESS

Pricing your customer and not your product implies that you have set up a structure that allows you to discriminate between different customers. The structure has two main components or tools: product packaging and pricing metrics.

Designing that structure is, to a large extent, what the rest of this book is about.

And it is, for the most part, exactly that: a design process. Sure, we can add a splash of quantitative data and advanced AI modeling here and there, but at the core of good pricing is the ability to create a framework of pricing that works—not something that is "optimal."

I usually use the example of the railroad to illustrate the process.

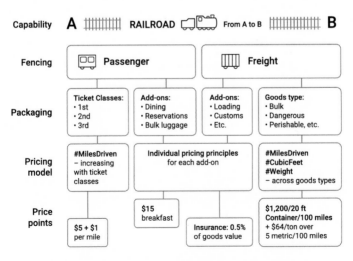

Figure 5: Simple overview of a pricing design flow for trains, capturing fencing, packaging, pricing model, and price points.

At the top, you have your capability: what your solution and organization can technically do for your customer. This is simply a collection of all the features, services, and terms and conditions you can—or could—put into a given offering to your customer.

From this follows a specific sequence of design questions you must answer, in order, before you should begin to even touch on the question of price points and "how much." You must have a solid structure in place that works both operationally and in sales, before you start optimizing it.

The structure is built by first separating your market into fences. For trains, that would be passenger and freight transportation as these are completely different markets served by your underlying capability.

Then, for each fence, you decide what is actually for sale. That is your packaging. Both fencing and packaging are covered in Chapter 3: Product Model.

Then comes the pricing model: how do you charge? It's not based on "how much." The customer cares a great deal about the "how," which is unpacked in Chapters 4 and 5: Pricing Model and Wallet Structuring.

Then, and only then, you can start building price points, which we will look at in Chapter 6: Price Points.

Once you are this far, you have to validate your new pricing with your customers, which we cover in Chapter 7: Validation.

In Chapter 8: Discounts, we talk about price execution and how to add discount model layers to your pricing architecture.

Chapter 9: Raising Prices, focuses on how you work with your prices over time as your product develops and how you keep track of which customers are closed on what pricing.

But first, we need to talk about how you start to build a

foundational understanding of the economics of the product you are creating to allow you to lay out a pricing strategy. We do this in Chapter 2: Scale Economics.

TWO

SCALE ECONOMICS

TYPES OF SCALE

THE THREE TYPES OF SCALE

Business is about selling something for a profit. Make it for a dime, sell it for a dollar. Do that enough times and you're rich. Simple.

SaaS has a special promise here: You can sell it twice (or 200 million times), but you only have to make it once. The costs sit at the overall product level—not at the unit level delivered to the customer. For that reason, it scales. It might cost $100 million to build a really top-notch, rich, and proven enterprise solution, but if you sell it to 5,000 customers for $100K each, you have a heck of a business, even if you have to spend another $100 million a year on overhead.

If you can get 5,000 customers, you can probably get 10,000, right? We've all heard and followed those stories.

However, with great profits come great competition. As soon as you've found an initial product-market fit, aligned all the parts of your commercial model, and have begun to really scale and hit that stride, some startup somewhere is pitching a VC with your logo at the bottom left of the "Competition" slide. Just as you did when you argued how you would have no trouble outcompeting all those old, dusty, outdated competitors whose solutions just didn't really solve the customers' problems like yours would.

If you can make it for a dime and sell it for a dollar, your competitor can also make it for a dime—and then decide to sell it for 90¢. Good for the customer. Bad for you. Hence, one of the iron laws of economics is that competition will eventually come for you and squeeze any profit margins you have down to the cost of capital. For that reason, the best definition I've ever heard of: "strategy" is "the plan you have to gain competitive advantage, defined as a sustainable way to keep profits above the cost of capital."

The profit formula is: unit price minus unit cost, minus overhead.

Your profit formula needs to be somehow better than your competitors—and not only them but also your future competitors. And also that startup with that "other idea" that suddenly gets funded $150 million to take you out. Or that huge legacy tech company that decides to enter your market, applying the full force of their ecosystem to crush your business model.

Even in those cases, your profit formula needs to outperform the cost of capital. Because if it does—especially if it obviously does, even as seen from the far distance of some VC partner meeting or a corporate strategy session—nobody will really want to throw capital at those competitors. Because how could anyone beat that superior model you've set up?

So how do you set up a superior profit formula? Well, you get scale at one of the stages of that formula:

1. Units sold: lower customer acquisition cost (CAC) than anyone else.

2. Unit price: higher product value than anyone else.

3. Unit cost: lower cost of delivering that product than anyone else.

Each of these categories has its own particular type of scale. Let's take a look at each of them, starting with the last one on the list: unit cost.

UNIT COST—ECONOMIES OF SCALE

The first type of scale that economic theory discovered was the scaling of production costs, and because it was the first, it was simply dubbed "economies of scale." The classic scenario is manufacturing: the cost per car if you build a million of them is way lower than if you build only 1,000.

That is built into most SaaS, as the cost to serve any single customer is probably very low. The true costs are the development of the product itself, costs of sale, and overhead. That's why we often talk about compounding in SaaS; add new customers every year, and sooner or later, you will hit break even, and then margins will rise fast from there. Whatever profit margin you have on the unit level (e.g., a 99 percent profit margin) is theoretically also the profit margin on the product or business level, if you can just manage to get all of the customers.

The problem with economies of scale in SaaS, however, is precisely that it scales so well. As we've already seen, if you're making something for ten cents and selling it for a dollar, there's nothing to stop your competitors from making it for the same price and undercutting you.

I serve as an advisor for HelloProper.com, a SaaS business that automates the administration of real estate residential rental units. They charge $15 per rental unit per month, but they have new entrants in their market that charge $5. If those new competitors can cover their overhead and development costs, their unit economics work out—they just need to reach scale.

In traditional manufacturing, where a product delivered to a customer actually costs something to make, economies of scale create a natural moat around your business. New competitors have to pay the initial high unit costs before they can reach scale. In SaaS, that moat is rarely there.

A good, recent example of economies of scale is cloud computing. AWS won that market with a very low-priced offering to reach economies of scale, burning through an initial period of negative margins on the first customers to achieve good margins on later customers.

The only real competitors in that market today are Alphabet's Google Cloud and Microsoft Azure—both produced by companies with enough funds to reach scale as well. I'd be hard-pressed to even imagine a business model that could provide cloud hosting and computing at a rate that could compete with those entrenched players—because it is in no way free to set up the infrastructure to serve those first customers.

UNIT PRICE—NETWORK EFFECTS

The second type of scale came a little later in the history of economics and is the increase of product value per unit as the number of units goes up, aptly named *network effects*.

The classic example of network effects is the telephone network: If you are the only person with a telephone, it has zero value. If there are two people with phones, well, now you can call each other. But if 1,000 people in your city have one, now it actually becomes valuable. If everyone else in the world has one, it becomes almost impossible to be the only one without one.

Facebook and other social media are modern examples of the same phenomenon: each new user adds value to the product itself.

The point is that the value of the product is above and beyond the costs sunk into its development. The code needed to support a million users is pretty much the same as the one needed to support one billion, but the latter product is far more valuable to those one billion users than the smaller, one-million niche product.

Lots of marketplace models have network effects: if you have only a few buyers and sellers, craigslist really isn't all that useful. But if you have all of the buyers and sellers, the value of selling your stuff on that platform is really high. Airbnb is another example of a marketplace with network effects.

UNITS SOLD—DISTRIBUTION EFFECTS AND VIRALITY

The last type of scale is scale of distribution, where the cost of sales per customer—your customer acquisition cost (CAC)—drops based on how many customers you have. Word of mouth, brand power, and viral marketing are versions of this, but the phenomenon is larger than all those elements.

I am an advisor to Contractbook, a series B legaltech startup that has a contract management and automation solution. One of their key acquisition strategies from the very beginning has been the viral effect that comes from customers sending contracts to non-customers, prompting them to create a free user profile and, hence, a lead to the sales team. The larger Contractbook grows, the cheaper their individual sales will be because more and more contracts are sent using their system.

The same dynamics have been in effect for pretty much all digital signature technologies since the beginning, as well as all other software that creates some form of interaction between customers.

Sometimes this interaction has to go through several "links" or types of users. For example, accounting software has very little inherent distribution effect between the businesses running it but quite a lot of distribution effect once it becomes the preferred system of an accountant who will then distribute it to all of his clients.

Branding is actually only a small part of this, although it is a significant one. Just think of a meditation app like Calm or Headspace. They are big B2C brands that *do* create market awareness and some word of mouth but not nearly in the same way as, say, a model like Zendesk, which by its design reaches many, many more people than just the users paying for it.

SCALE COMBINATIONS

If you can combine types of scale, you have something really good.

Facebook is a great example. Its model has the same inherent cost scaling as most other SaaS companies: the Nth user is far cheaper to serve than the first one. It also has product scale due to the network effect, where more users equal more value for those users (rendering the product more valuable overall).

That is true not only for the users of Facebook but also for its customers, namely the advertisers. If everyone is on Facebook, I not only get to target the whole world with my advertising, but the targeting algorithms are also way better, and I get to fine slice my market much more precisely, creating a higher ROI on my marketing.

Finally, Facebook also has scale of distribution, both on a user and a customer level. I was in my twenties in 2007 when Facebook swept across the world. I still remember that hype; suddenly everyone had an account. It was cool and free, so why not? Then six months later, my grandmother had one.

When they finally figured out that their business model was to make money on advertising, every agency in the world (another user type) got on board to sell the power of Facebook to their customers (i.e., every B2C business from Alaska to Zimbabwe).

Facebook is striking because the rate of scale was so enormous early on, especially the scale of distribution. Between February 2004 and the end of December 2007, the company went from one account (Mark Zuckerberg's own) to fifty-eight million monthly users (my grandmother among them). Four years later, they were pushing toward a billion.

A lot of other SaaS businesses have scale combinations too, albeit at a lower rate. Most development tools, for example, enjoy scale of product and distribution through their users. As more and more developers use something (Jira, GitHub, Bitpanda, Twilio— take your pick), those same developers will move around from organization to organization, from project to project, and use those same tools over and over again. If they are hired in development bureaus or agencies, those tools will become standards used on all customer projects. Because that is how economies of scale are deployed on the agency level: use a few tools for everything.

As more and more developers learn to use a tool, that tool becomes more valuable to the customers—who, mind you, are not the developers but their employers. That's because it's much easier to hire developers to work with a tool that loads of people know compared to a new one that nobody has ever heard of.

Every time real scale is reached, a competitive advantage is potentially there to be had. Without it, growth becomes too expensive. Yes, as a SaaS business, you will have economies of scale, but so will everyone else. Without scale of product or scale of distribution, you are unlikely to create a profit model that deters potential competitors.

In the following sections, we'll first unpack the unit mathematics of scale; then we'll cover some scale dynamics that are key to understand, before looking at a design framework to map out how you can build scale into your product ecosystem.

SAAS ECONOMICS: CLTV/CAC

SAAS ECONOMICS

Remember when I said a strategy is "a plan for how to be more profitable than your competition?"

Time to unpack that.

Remember, your superior profit model needs either one or more of the following: 1) lower CAC; 2) lower product cost, or, if all else fails; 3) lower delivery costs. And these need to improve as you scale.

The financial metric I use as the core yardstick of profitability is the CLTV/CAC ratio.[5] I also often use it as tracking to ensure I've created value during a pricing project.

---

5 CLTV is customer lifetime value and is the (average revenue per account – development and delivery costs)/ churn rate: (ARPA – DDC)/CHURN percentage. CAC is "customer acquisition cost" and is the average money spent on acquiring a new customer.

The components of CLTV are average revenue per account (ARPA), development and delivery costs (DDC), churn rate, and customer acquisition cost (CAC):

$$\frac{(ARPA - DDC)/CHURN\%}{CAC} = \frac{CLTV}{CAC}$$

Figure 6: The CLTV/CAC formula captures the ratio between the cost of acquiring a customer and the total lifetime gross profits of that customer.

CLTV IS THE KEY FORMULA FOR UNIT ECONOMICS

At its core, the CLTV/CAC formula tells you how many dollars of net revenue you get for every one dollar you spend on sales and marketing. Net revenue, obviously, is the revenue that's left after your immediate costs are taken out.

So a CLTV/CAC of "5" means that over the course of the customers' lifetime—taken as an average of all your customers—you will earn five dollars after costs for every one dollar you spend on acquiring those customers.

The formula is powerful because it captures all the relevant aspects of the unit economics in a SaaS business, ignoring overhead because economies of scale are already assumed in a SaaS business.

There is no real market consensus on how to calculate CLTV/CAC. I, for example, subtract both development and delivery costs on a unit basis. Most others would consider development as part of overhead, which is a fair argument, especially when you are considering early-stage startups. For more mature companies, however, continuous, budgeted development just becomes a way of life—year after year. While there is some cost scaling, it's not as pretty as it appears on most early-stage founder Excel sheets, so I usually include it.

Others will argue about how to calculate CAC. If 40 percent of your staff are salespeople, should 40 percent of your HR costs go into CAC? Should you include customers who churn immediately in the calculation? Until there is some official, unified understanding of how to make the calculation, just pick one that fits your business, stick to that, and be transparent about it.

COMPETITIVE PRESSURE AND DYNAMICS INSIDE THE CLTV/CAC FORMULA

The CLTV/CAC ratio has been around for a while, but SaaS businesses often fail to appreciate that their CLTV/CAC ratio is under competitive pressure. Let's look into that.

ARPA is essentially a function of what your customers are willing to pay for your product. If ARPA is high compared to your competition, it's probably because you have a great product and great service, which means high development and delivery costs, especially long term. So the two things cancel each other out.

Your customer acquisition cost, meanwhile, is directly competing with the costs spent by your competitors to acquire those same customers. If it's low, then perhaps you're underpricing (i.e., low ARPA), and your CAC would normalize if you dared price at value for your product. Or your product is great and innovative and is commanding the attention of the customers, enabling you to either charge a premium or sell cheaply. But what is the guarantee that this is sustainable? What is the guarantee that in four years you won't be pulled apart by twenty new, venture-backed competitors and five corporate ventures, all dying to hit those same numbers?

The three types of scale covered in the previous section each target a specific component of this profitability formula.

Cost scaling targets development and delivery costs (DDC). As you go further and further into economies of scale on the cost side, your gross margins will increase. While development costs do increase as your product and business grows, they don't increase at the rate of your revenue. You will also get better pricing on a lot of your input costs, unit for unit.

Product scaling is more universal. Since it simply increases product value, you get to decide how this applies in your case. Do you raise prices but then remain at a similar CAC? Or do you keep your pricing but then enjoy lower CAC as your offering is now a better value? Or do you reduce development costs, banking on the influx of users to create the future value of the product instead of continuously pushing for new features, better design, and so on?

Distribution scaling, of course, targets your CAC, lowering it for each additional customer your product gets on board.

So cost scaling targets the numerator, distribution scaling targets the denominator, and product scaling can target either of the two, depending on how you apply it to your business model. What you should choose depends on your competitive circumstances and what scale dynamics are in your market. If, for example, you are in a winner-takes-all market, you should probably lower CAC as much as possible to grow your market share.

SCALE CURVES: COMPOUNDING, CRITICAL MASS, PLATEAUS, AND WINNER TAKES ALL

Not all scaling is created equal. Some products produce value for the customer right out of the gate and then just build from there.

Other products have a "chicken and egg" dynamic, where you first need a critical mass to really make the product attractive. Other products—like Facebook—have all of the scale. (But then it turns out that the social media market actually wasn't a winner takes all, and a plethora of other options could spring up with just as much success and provide real competition for Facebook. Apparently, we can have profiles in more places than one.)

One way to predict how a SaaS business will do is to understand what kind of scaling will happen and how those unit economics will develop as it grows. Another way is to understand the market dynamics around that business and what competitive situation they will create.

Let's look at the different types of scaling with a few visuals.

LINEAR SCALING

Linear scaling is when scale happens from the very first unit and then continues forever from there, like this:

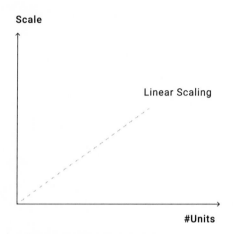

Figure 7: Linear scaling is the improvement of economics at a constant rate as the volume of units increases.

For every order of magnitude of size you achieve, you create a similar order of magnitude of impact on the scaling in question. For cost scaling, if you 10x the users, then you 1/10x the cost per unit. For distribution scaling, if you 10x the customers, then you've reduced your CAC.

Now, the scaling doesn't have to be 1:1. It's still linear scaling if every doubling of your size only improves your scale by 0.25. The main point is that it's still going to be a 0.25 improvement of the unit of scale when you double again. And again.

Reid Hoffmann (of LinkedIn fame) was the first to really point this out with his book *Blitzscaling*. If you google "blitzscaling Google" or "blitzscaling Amazon" you can find nice graphs depicting their revenue growth and various costs' growth over time. You can see remarkably consistent linearity between these, going from a few million in annual recurring revenue (ARR) to multiple billion.

CRITICAL MASS

Critical mass scaling is the tough scenario where nothing happens until everything happens all at once, like this:

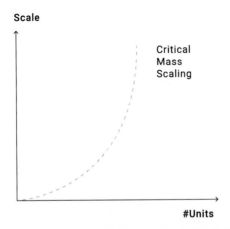

Figure 8: Critical mass scaling is the improvement of economics at an accelerating rate as the volume of units increases, often involving a tipping point.

Here, the rate of scale is really low initially until suddenly a tipping point is reached and the rate of scale accelerates with each new unit added.

Most marketplaces, but not all, have a similar scaling dynamic around product-value scaling. If you invite buyers and sellers into a marketplace with only very few other buyers and sellers, the value of that marketplace is very low. But suddenly you have enough, and value starts to build faster. You have reached critical mass in that market.

That is why most marketplaces—from Airbnb to dating websites to craigslist to Amazon—usually start out by owning a niche. Airbnb started in New York, dating websites go local and target a particular segment of users (and most use fake profiles or bots to fill up their website until they hit an actual critical mass of real users). Craigslist started as a local newsletter in San Francisco. Amazon started with books and got good at that before it branched out.

Critical mass is real. If you bite off more than you can chew, you end up with nothing. Zilch. And you only have to miss by a little bit to have the result go to zero.

DIMINISHING RETURNS

Another scaling dynamic is the one where initial scaling is linear but then drops off at a certain level—like a reverse critical mass.

The effect is some form of saturation or fulfillment of an underlying requirement.

I once worked with a large industrial company in Germany (to remain unnamed) that created a software platform for their own factories to have a real-time overview of all the spare parts that were in inventory across all their locations. In that way, they could optimize spare parts purchasing because each location didn't have to buy their own, as long as they had an overview of what was available in the network.

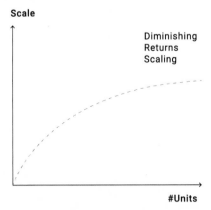

Figure 9: Diminishing returns scaling is the decelerating rate of improvement of economics as volume of units increases past a certain point.

Here, scale happens as soon as you link up two locations. And three is better than two. And four is better than three. But it turned out that after about five or six locations, there wasn't much more optimization to be had. Distances became too large between locations, and inventory couldn't be reduced much more. Product value scaling topped out pretty quickly and then flatlined.

WINNER TAKES ALL

In some markets, there can be only one. You only need one search engine, for example. So even when Bing! came along with huge backing from Microsoft, it could barely dent the market share of Google.

Microsoft's Office Suite with Word and Excel had an effective monopoly for nearly two decades. It took a massive player like

Alphabet to offer a free product in Google Docs and Google Sheets, and keep pushing them and developing them for years, to make a small dent in Microsoft's market share. Apparently, word and number processing is a winner-takes-all market as well.

The underlying dynamics are whether the product you are pushing into the market is of a complementary or a substitute nature, combined with whether there are real dynamics of scale, especially on the product value side.

If your product is complementary to other products, customers can enjoy it and the similar offerings of your competitors. That is the case with social media, for example. You can have both Facebook and Instagram, which is why Facebook bought IG. They had no way to kill it, even though they had 100 percent of the market. It was simply a new, complementary product that was going to live side-by-side with Facebook.

That is the kicker with complementary products: no matter how much they scale, it really doesn't hurt your competition that much. There is room for several adjacent offerings in the market.

A substitute product, however, is one where it only makes sense to have one, like accounting software, a payroll system, or a CRM platform.

QuickBooks, for example, has an 80 percent share of their target small- and medium-size businesses (SMB) segment of the market in the US. And they have a very nice profit margin of 26 percent, which on $10 billion in ARR is not bad.

But it has taken QuickBooks, which was founded in 1983, forty years to reach that size. It is a winner-takes-all market, yes, and there are some decent cost scaling and some decent distribution scaling built into the model, yes, but they are not great. Most of it is just pure, hard work and staying power in the market.

Google Search—and the audience for AdWords that it created—had a unique combination of winner-takes-all dynamics and very good cost and product value scaling. Once AdWords was established as a category, marketing agencies around the world were ready to distribute it as part of their services.

THAT IS WHY YOU SHOULD HAVE A PRICING STRATEGY

So we have three types of scaling: cost, product, and distribution. We also have three curve dynamics: linear, critical mass, and diminishing. And, finally, we have the substitute/complementary distinction that governs whether a product—once scaled—will keep competition away. Having a clear and realistic view of the dynamics of your SaaS business across these scale dimensions will give you an insight into how you can reach a point where you enjoy a true competitive advantage (i.e., sustainable high profits).

"Strategy" is simply your plan for how to get there, so your "pricing strategy" should be an extension and booster of your overall strategy. For instance, if you know you have product-value dynamics the more users you have, and you can turn those users into a product you can sell to another audience of customers—just like Facebook has turned us all into marketing audiences—then it's probably a good idea to have a freemium model. If you are facing a scenario with critical mass scaling of product value, then a land-and-expand strategy, where you get customers in very cheaply and quickly and raise prices later on, might be right for you.

And so on. Pricing strategy follows business strategy, and business strategy is a plan for how to enjoy sustainable high-profit margins. Scale is the only way to do that.

THE CUPID MODEL: DESIGNING FOR SCALE

CUPID

When helping SaaS companies with their strategies, I often use a framework to design their product ecosystem around the three types of scale.

Enter the CUPID model of SaaS strategy.

CUPID is an acronym for:

- Customers
- Users
- Product
- Iteration
- Distribution

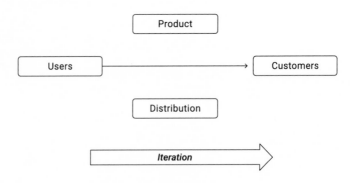

Figure 10: The CUPID model is a framework to understand the current and potential scaling dynamics in your product ecosystem.

The key question the CUPID model forces you to answer is "What is the value path from user to customer?" Or, put another way, how do we turn the value your software creates in the world into cold, hard cash in your pocket?

The CUPID model helps you answer the value-path question because it forces you to view your users as only one of three things: your customers, your product, or your distributors.

Your users are never "just users." They are either users who pay you (called customers), users who bring other types of users to you, who then pay you (making them distributors), or users who, by their use, become something you can repackage and sell to someone else (making them the product).

Let's look at each of these categories in turn.

USERS AS CUSTOMERS

If your users are your customers, that's straightforward. They like your product, so they pay to use it. Every CEO and VC partner will understand that.

I call that a "straight-arrow CUPID" because there is a direct relationship between the primary value your software delivers and what your customers are willing to pay for.

Figure 11: The first of the three potential roles the user has is simply that of being the customer.

For example, Tame.events sells a suite of event-management software to businesses who want to organize events, from 3M to your local charity. The value of the product is that it saves you a massive amount of time and stress and increases the production value of your event. And both 3M and your local charity know that, so they pay. Easy.

As long as Tame keeps increasing the value of its primary software solution and selling to new customers every year, it will grow. Its margins will grow too.

That's iteration. If you run the "script" of your business multiple times, then what? For Tame, as it gets more users, it gets more customers. Customers pay the bills and generate profit. Cost scaling is realized. Great!

So when your user is your customer, it's straightforward—you just keep strengthening that relationship as much as you can.

USERS AS PRODUCT

Sometimes your users are not your customers; sometimes they are your product. This is the model of classic radio: the stations put up a great program to get you to tune in, and then they aggregate you and all the other listeners as an audience and sell you to advertisers. It's Facebook's business model when they sell your love for cat memes to Nestlé's pet food division.

You—the user—are the product.

Figure 12: The user can also be the product itself, like Facebook's user being audiences sold to advertisers.

For example, BeMyEyes.com is an app that creates a video link between a visually impaired person and a random volunteer who can then help them "see" through the video link. Stuff like,

"Is this a can of beans or tomatoes?" Or "Which blouse goes with these pants?" Or "Please tell me how many lines appeared on this home pregnancy test."

Blind and visually impaired people often stop asking relatives mundane questions in order to not constantly bother them and to make room in their close relationships for conversations that are not (for once) centered on their disability. So Be My Eyes was an instant global success. It quickly became the world's largest community of visually impaired people, with a total of over six million users and around ten volunteers for every visually impaired person.

But how do you monetize that? Do you charge the visually impaired a monthly subscription? How will the volunteers feel about that? Or the visually impaired? Okay, do you then charge the visually impaired *less*? To piss off everyone *less*? Can you get volunteers to micro-pay to help? Maybe, but you'd run a potentially irreparable reputation risk if you tried it out. And, even if it works, it's unlikely to be a huge commercial success.

No. You decide that the users are not the customers.

It's immediately obvious that running the world's largest community of visually impaired people and millions of phone calls with volunteers explaining visual images in over 150 languages is somehow *valuable*. So your users are—simply by using your basic solution—becoming your product. You just need to figure out who wants to buy it. (And how to package it for them.)

You ask yourself the iteration question: "What will happen over time if we keep doing this?" If we keep adding these users-who-are-not-customers, then what product is created that gives us a clear path to our real customers?

Be My Eyes decided to allow large corporations (including

Microsoft, Google, and Lloyds Bank) to interface with the app and provide customer service to visually impaired users directly from the app. And it charged them for it.

So by building a user base and delivering to them for free, Be My Eyes was able to turn that base into the core value of the product that it then sold to its real customers: multinational organizations who care about their CSR profile and want to provide equal access to their support staff for everyone.

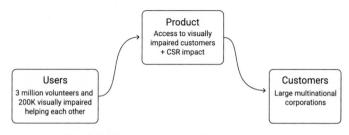

Figure 13: BeMyEyes' users are a key part of the product value being sold to their corporate customers.

The next step for Be My Eyes now (apart from making the world a more friendly place for the visually impaired, of course) is to increase the value of their product by providing their new customers with a suitable software suite of functionality. So this becomes their product roadmap: building web apps for support staff and integrating the apps' video connections with existing support software, etc. While, of course, ensuring that their community of visually impaired users keeps growing.

USERS AS DISTRIBUTION

Sometimes, your users are neither your customers nor your product. That happens when it's not immediately clear that you can aggregate them into something valuable. However, you might be able to use them as a distribution channel to get to another type of customer, who you can charge for a solution.

Figure 14: The user can also be the de facto distribution, thus lowering CAC as the user base grows.

For example, KNIME.com is an open-source data-analytics platform. Its users are data scientists—in the broadest possible sense of that term—who are looking for tools to create value from all their data. It has hundreds of thousands of those users.

KNIME's customers, however, are large multinationals like Proctor & Gamble, who install KNIME in an on-prem or private cloud and then use it to run all sorts of internal data processes, from single-insight-type analyses to standardized reporting up, down, and across their organization. While P&G would, of course, employ data scientists to run KNIME on their internal use case, the features they need are distinctly different from those of the open-source user (e.g., operational security, audit trails, advanced roles and permissions). KNIME can create a whole lot of value for a customer like Proctor & Gamble, which means that its price, possibly, should try and aim for a share of that value.

That, again, means the sales process to sell KNIME to a corporate client like P&G is no small feat—business cases have to be built. You'd have to meet with several internal teams and executives up and down the corporate ladder, and the process can take years.

CAC (customer acquisition costs, remember) will, consequently, be sky high.

That is exactly why KNIME is so invested in its open-source platform. Because among those 100,000s of freeloading open-source users is a senior data scientist in Proctor & Gamble who gets to try out the core functionality of the product (data analytics) and grows to like it before she eventually suggests internally that P&G starts using KNIME.

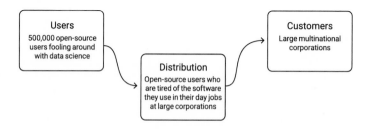

Figure 15: KNIME's open-source users are a key driver of the distribution of KNIME's enterprise solutions.

That enables KNIME to sell to large corporates like P&G at a fraction of the cost compared to its competitors, who spend years in conference rooms with slide decks trying to convince the same customers to buy.

Another example, Peergrade.io is a piece of software that allows university professors to distribute the job of grading essays to the students themselves. So as a student, I now log onto a platform and am randomly assigned feedback tasks on two to four anonymized essays from other students in my class, and consequently, I will get feedback from two to four of my peers on my own essay.

Sounds good, right? Students learn more, and professors don't have to read 300 undergrad papers. Everybody wins. Except Peergrade, because the students don't want to pay, and university professors don't have any money.

So it uses the professors as a distribution channel to sell to its real customers: the universities. The model is similar to KNIME: give low-priced and/or free versions of the software to the users (the professors) and then use the users as distribution to reach your customer.

The users-as-distributors model requires two elements to work: a push and a pull.

First, the push. The structure of your use case for the basic user has to somehow reach your real customer. For KNIME, that happens because the data scientists love the product and prompt their managers to buy the real version so they can use it on internal projects.

For Peergrade, it happens because universities discover that their professors are running student data on an external system, which they just can't tolerate. That prompts the universities to ask the professors to stop using Peergrade, which they don't want to do. So there is some internal conflict that results in the professors arguing for an institution-wide adoption of Peergrade, which is how the sales process is started.

Second, the pull. The solution you've built offers some benefits to the customer above and beyond what the primary user needs. For KNIME, that is operational scalability, audit trails, security, and all the other enterprise software features that aren't relevant for individual data scientists or small teams. For Peergrade, it's integration into learning management systems, institution dashboards, and other features that aren't relevant for individual professors.

A PUSH AND A PULL

For the users-as-distributor model to work, you need both a push and a pull factor. You need a reason for the users to tell the customer they need to buy and a bonus for the customer if they do so.

If you miss the push effect, you are just going to have a lot of happy, non-paying users, and you can join the graveyard of SaaS companies that committed suicide with an ill-designed freemium model (or an open-source that never managed to monetize or some other failed upgrade path).

If you miss the pull effect, your customer will be reluctant to buy—why should they?—because your product will not seem like it's built to accommodate the value creation that the customer is seeking. It will seem like it's built for non-professional data science teams or for individual professors, not for big and serious organizations with all the product demands that entails.

ITERATION

Which brings us to iteration. What happens if you "run the script" of your user-case multiple times? What happens when the professors actually like the product and start using it? What happens when the open-source community grows? What happens when—as with Tame—you suddenly have a large pool of customers who organize events through your software?

Well, your strategic options open up. You get to pursue new paths to either existing or new customers—perhaps even with stronger distribution (i.e., lower acquisition costs) or stronger product (i.e., higher value and pricing power).

Let's look at Tame as an example. At its core, this is its strategy:

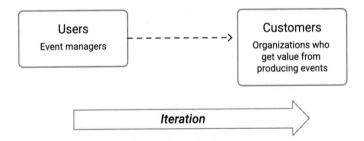

Figure 16: Iteration is the addition of time to the user-customer relationship, which is what generates scale through compounding.

Users get value from the product and buy it. If Tame is successful in creating and repeating this dynamic, it will get more users and, hence, more customers.

That opens up a further step in their iteration.

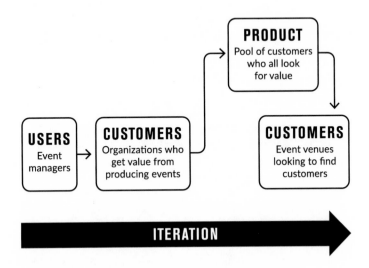

Figure 17: TAME's first customers—event managers—will compound through iteration to become another product for a second group of customers—venues—over time, the first with linear scale, the second with critical mass scaling.

If Tame manages to get a lot of customers who are all producing events, then that starts to be a valuable resource Tame can monetize. So while the core user is also the core customer, over time this "customer" also turns into a "product" for another customer: the event venues, who are all looking for ways to find events to host.

If Tame gets that far, that opens up another iterative dynamic.

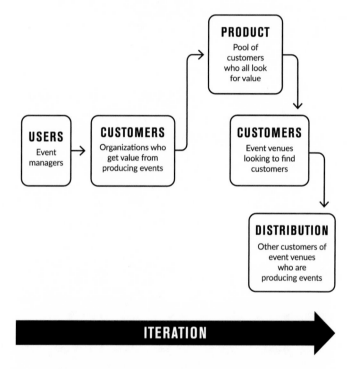

Figure 18: TAME's venue customers will now become a distribution channel for their first customer base, the event managers. Thus the product ecosystem has reached circularity and can grow on its own, assuming critical mass is reached and TAME properly manages the quality and operations of each link.

If it manages to onboard the event venues to its platform, then Tame can build functionality for those venues, such as digitalized floorplans that make it even easier for the event managers of the core customers to choose their particular venue. That, in turn, can be used as an incentive for the venues to just push this digital version to new non-Tame event managers, effectively working as distributors of Tame to new potential core customers.

Another strategy for Tame to pursue after the initial user-customer iteration is the speaker marketplace.

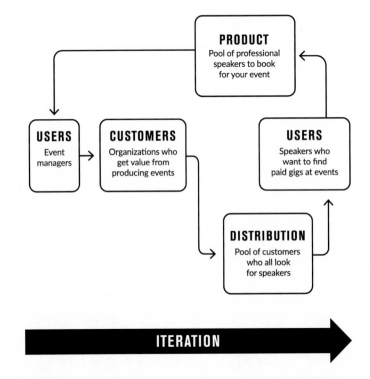

Figure 19: TAME has a second path to circularity through creating a speaker marketplace.

Once they have enough customers who organize events and upload bios and pictures of the speakers at these events, it's relatively easy for Tame to use this flow of information to reach out to all those speakers and ask them if they would like—for free—to be part of an internal marketplace of speakers.

Once that marketplace is set up, Tame can offer it to their core customers—many of whom are likely happy to get rid of expensive and old-fashioned speaker agencies. Tame can then charge a commission from the customers based on the speakers' fees (just as the agencies do).

PRICING POWER AND ACQUISITION COSTS

Each connector arrow is an iteration: "do this multiple times, then that happens." But it also resembles a part of both your product model and your pricing model. Or, rather, for it to properly work, it requires that your product model and pricing model properly support that iteration step.

So to go from "user" to "customer," Tame needs a product model that fits the use case of its customers and a pricing model that charges for that use. If Tame gives it away for free, then it doesn't have the user-as-customer connection.

Similar to the venue strategy, Tame needs a product model that properly aggregates the customers in a format that can be sold to the venues: the second customer. And it needs a pricing model that captures value from this aggregation.

Finally, Tame also needs a product model that makes it easy for the venues to onboard new non-Tame users and a pricing model that doesn't block this distribution step. One way to do that is by making it free (it just makes good sense for the venues to use one software platform instead of many). Another way is to incentivize the venues (this could be in the form of kickbacks, not charging for the referral of a venue-customer in the form of you-send-me-one-I-send-you-one, providing access to premium features of the product, etc.).

Again, every arrow needs to be supported by both your product model (how your solution works) and your pricing model (what and how you charge). It's the proper combination of product and pricing that enables you to transition from one box to the other.

If you manage—like in the two-example strategy cases with Tame, above—to build a loop where either product or distribution loops back to your original user or customer, then good things will happen. A product loop will increase the value of your product and the price you can charge over time.

As we have seen, that is what's called a "network effect" in economic theory. It's the network effect that makes social media worthless if you're the only one on it and worth billions if everyone uses it.

Some network effects are linear: adding value from the start and incrementally as new users or customers are onboarded. This is the case, for example, with private executive networks. The value of a network group doesn't rise exponentially as you go from a twelve-person group to a twenty-four-person group.

Other network effects are exponential: adding value at a faster and faster degree as users or customers are onboarded. This is the case with LinkedIn, for example. Although my private network doesn't double in value as I go from 500 to 1,000 connections, my value from LinkedIn's perspective rises as they manage to cover a larger and larger percentage of every professional on the planet.[6]

A distribution loop works similarly to a product loop, but instead of a network effect of increased product value and future pricing

---

6   Or, perhaps more correctly, my value from joining any other online networking platform drops as LinkedIn's market share rises. Because why would I join another networking platform when everyone is on LinkedIn?

power, a distribution loop lowers your acquisition cost, making the next users or customers cheaper to acquire.

A distribution loop like Tame's venue strategy isn't clearly exponential in nature. The first venue you get on board that starts to spread the word isn't worth less than the one-hundredth one. But each one refers users as customers to you in the form of event managers and their organizations.

OK, BUT WHERE THE HELL IS THE PRICING?

As I mentioned previously, for the dynamics of the CUPID model to work, you need the iteration steps (i.e., each connector arrow) to be supported by both the product model and the pricing model. We will cover that in detail in later chapters.

That said, here are the guidelines for pricing in the CUPID model:

- User-as-customer: charge for value delivered
- User-as-product: give it away for free
- User-as-distribution: pay them

To see those rules in action, let's take a look at Tame's venue strategy again.

Let's unpack this step by step.

You charge the users as customers according to value delivered (we cover competition later).

Once you have enough of these customers, you aggregate them into a product you can sell to venues. You will probably not be able to charge for this, so you offer it to your customers for free.

You charge the venues based on the value of these aggregated event managers. However, you also want the venues to distribute your software for you, so you do everything you can across both product and pricing to incentivize them. You make it easy for them and provide them with a new revenue stream of kickbacks as they push your software to their customers.

You provide these new customers with easy access to your software to showcase the value to them (this can be free trials, freemium versions, or a version of the software where you grant them access as sub-users via the venue's account). Regardless of the actual execution, the purpose is the same: get these prospects to experience the value as users so they will want to become paying customers.

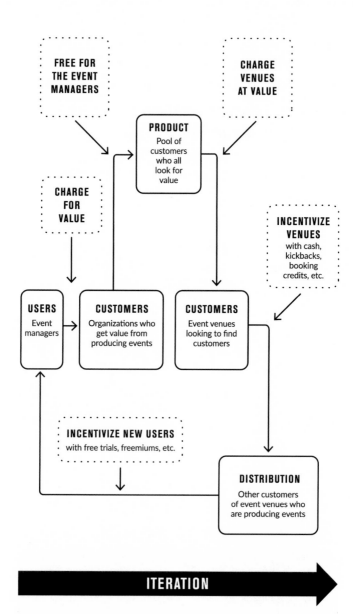

Figure 20: Pricing is a key part of ensuring the flow at each individual link of the CUPID model in order to create flow-through and scale at the overall model level.

FREQUENT PRICING MISTAKES:
CODE-X CHARGING THEIR DISTRIBUTORS

One of the most frequent pricing mistakes I see is SaaS businesses trying to charge their distributors—essentially demanding to get paid to get customers.

Case in point: I was working with Code-X (*real name withheld*)—a corporate spin-off in the logistics sector that creates a unified API that connects logistics partners (think of a chain of fifty warehouses across Europe with fifty different IT systems) with e-commerce businesses looking for a large-scale logistics provider (think of an online store with +€1M in revenue). An integration before Code-X could easily cost €50,000, which was prohibitive for 90 percent of the e-commerce stores. That meant lost business for the logistics providers and lost efficiency of scale for the e-commerce stores.

Through interviews, Code-X had good validation that the logistics providers would pay to have the API front to their systems so they could serve the long tail of e-commerce stores. Maybe something like €1,000 per warehouse per month. Or maybe €500.

But this left a big question: why would the warehouses go through the trouble of trying to convert all customers who had already paid €50,000 for an integration to the Code-p API?

Simple. The warehouses are not your customers; they are your distributors. Pay them a kickback on revenue generated from onboarding e-commerce stores and have the e-commerce stores pay a few cents per package handled in an "API fee."

For the warehouses, there was a meaningful difference between being charged €1,000 a month for an API they would have to earn back via a razor-thin operating margin on serving smallish e-commerce stores and being paid to actively reduce IT complexity while opening up new, more profitable customer streams. So they went for it. And for Code-X, the entire go-to-market game shifted entirely.

Takeaway: if you want your distributors to move your product, pay them.

That's what the CUPID model lays out. It showcases the economic dynamics going forward for your product and starts to track how you create a better CLTV/CAC ratio:

- Every straight arrow (users as customers) produces economies of scale through increasingly better unit economics for every new customer.

- Every "up-arrow" (users as product) produces product-value-scaling opportunities that increase product value and are, therefore, essentially free development costs you can convert into revenue with a straight arrow.

- Every "down-arrow" (users as distribution) produces distribution scaling and reduces the cost of acquiring new customers and users.

The rule of thumb is that a good SaaS business has all three types of arrows: straight revenue generators, up-sloping product-value generators, and down-sloping distribution dynamics. The great SaaS businesses make the "up arrows" and the "down arrows" loop back along the chain to create a feedback loop that just builds and builds with each iteration.

STRATEGY: BUSINESS AND PRICING

So to recap, you need a plan to make a profit model that beats the competition. Consistently.

That plan comes from carefully using your product model and your pricing model to actively create product value and distribution power at low costs and claim fair value through pricing once you've reached the customer. At one step in your CUPID flow, a land-and-expand strategy might be completely right, but you should know why. Are you building product value or distribution? When do you reach the next stage? How should your product model and pricing model be set up then to move you forward?

We will cover the product model and pricing models in the next two chapters. Next up is Chapter 3, which deals with how to structure your product model to target core sources of demand and discriminate between customers so you reach prices they are each willing and happy to pay.

THREE

PRODUCT MODEL

PACKAGING IS YOUR FIRST TOOL TO PRICE THE CUSTOMER

Your product model is what you decide to sell to whom. It's what
your customers buy from you in the broadest possible sense: the
technical and functional features of your software or technology, the
service and organization you wrap around it, and the commercial
features (e.g., free trials, tie-in periods, payment terms). At a high
level, this is the dynamics of your product ecosystem, which is the
"product" part of how all the arrows in the CUPID model work.

TWO LEVELS: PRODUCT ECOSYSTEM AND PACKAGING

In the last chapter, I introduced you to Tame.events. Let's now take
it as an example again. Tame creates something to sell to event
managers and then, later on, creates something to sell to venues,
then speakers, and so on.

Think of this as the distinction between running passenger
trains to California while also transporting mail for the US Postal
Service in a safe in the locomotive—or even establishing a freight

train service to transport heavy goods. The passenger train is your first product. It drives the investment in the rail line and the expansion of your network, and you can then add revenue streams to that infrastructure by transporting other things.

All these things have to support each other in such a way as to build more value than your costs of delivery and development would warrant—or create distribution mechanisms to reduce your customer acquisition costs. Or both. Only when one of these dynamics is in place (increased product value or decreased acquisition costs) can you scale and turn a dollar of cost into more dollars of profit than your competitors.

This is exactly the "eco" part of "product ecosystem." It's the interplay and "larger-than-the-sum-of-its-parts" that should work, not some particular feature or subset.

At the more granular level of your product model, you have your specific use cases and value propositions. This is where Tame tries to convince event managers to buy its event-management software and where the trains create a first-, second-, and third -class ticket structure for passengers.

So far, at this level of granularity, we are still using design thinking. We are trying to be "roughly right" in our overall understanding of which customers to serve and how. We will worry about nitty-gritty feature selection and bundling later on. Big picture first.

FENCING AND LADDERING

I usually work with two overarching design principles to help tech businesses design their product models at this level:

1. **Fencing:** the separation of your customers into overall different categories (e.g., train passengers vs. freight transportation).[7]

2. **Laddering:** the product structure within a fence that guides the customers' purchase, usage, expansion of that purchase, usage over time, and finally the price they pay (e.g., first-, second-, and third-class ticket structure for passengers).

All levels of your product model need to be supported and integrated into pricing models (which we'll cover in the next chapter).

FENCING

Fencing is the first "price-your-customer" decision you have to make when designing your commercial model. It's the top-level segmentation of customers into different product and pricing schemes to better deliver and extract value.

Let me give an example.

I worked with a Danish series A startup that had created a subscription service for laboratory thermal monitoring. At the base of the service are small, high-tech thermometers that automatically send temperature logs via the local Wi-Fi to the cloud and then back to a web app, where the laboratory compliance team can then check the calibration history and certificates of all their active thermal units.

The startup sends the labs new thermometers whenever the

---

7 If you are a seasoned pricing or revenue management professional, you probably use the word "fencing" differently—more as a catch-all term for various methods that allow for price discrimination. However, I've found it to be an easily graspable way to describe the process of categorizing customers when creating a product model.

old ones are up for recalibration, along with a return envelope where the labs can just chuck their old thermometers. They then get recalibrated (or recycled) at the startups' own thermal lab. The value proposition is clear: the laboratories save a ton of money and time and don't have to carefully create a compliance process around their thermal monitoring because the startup has already done that for them.

Great. Except it turned out that it was relatively hard to sell to labs.

When I talked to Adam, the CEO, he said something along the lines of "We sell these thermometer subscriptions. But the food laboratories are very price sensitive and generally don't buy into the cost or time savings. They usually simply throw thermometers away and buy new ones. On the other hand, we also sell to large pharma companies—and here we have the sense that we are so cheap that they don't trust that our service really works."

The solution: don't sell them the same product. By trying to create a value proposition combining technical product features, services, pricing, and marketing messages that hit two such different customer types, you've created a nearly unsolvable problem for yourself.

It's much easier to split the problem into two—the pharma problem and the food problem—and then solve each one on its own, which is easier and produces a better result. Then all you have to do is make sure that customers know which category they belong to and that they don't cross over.

That's fencing.

We created a black "Food Unit" for the startup to sell to food laboratories and a white "Pharma Unit" that sold at five times the price to pharma laboratories. All the surrounding services, ISO standards, etc. were then sprinkled over the value propositions to support each.

Another example is Zoom. If you look at the pricing page of Zoom, you will see they separate their product into the fences: all, education, healthcare, and developers. They do this because developers need a completely different product from Zoom; they want a technical toolbox they can use to develop something else. Healthcare and education are the two main verticals in the US that traditionally have a lot of volume but also a low willingness to pay compared to everyone else (i.e., all).

FENCING ALLOWS PRICING AND PRODUCT SPECIALIZATION

Inside the fences, you get to have distinctly different product and pricing models. If you have fenced B2C and B2B separately, for instance, then you can deliver one product to consumers and charge them in a particular way and do something completely different for businesses—without either one of these fences likely worrying about this too much.

That is the strength of fencing: because a well-designed fence allows you to do different things on both the product and the pricing levels, and you can better fit both product and pricing to the customers in each fence. That turns into more cost-effective sales and an ability to price more closely to each customer's willingness to pay.

Fencing is your first and primary tool in your pricing toolbox. The first question you try to answer when considering pricing should be: "Is there an obvious way to separate our customers into distinct categories that will make all subsequent packaging and pricing easier?"

Now, let's dig into a few particulars that will help you create good fences.

The rules of fencing are that each fence should be:

1. **Discreet:** must be clearly definable by both you and your customers.

2. **Stable:** must be "unjumpable."

3. **Fair:** should, in most cases, be seen as fair enough to be publicly available.

4. **Obvious:** if it feels awkward, it probably is.

5. **Valuable:** should provide a minimum +30 percent CLTV/CAC contrast to be worth it.

Let's review them one at a time, before taking a look at a sample list of fences.

Discreet: To work properly, a fence should be measurable and non-arbitrary so both you and your customers can determine instantly in which category they belong. It also means the delineation between the categories should, preferably, be determined outside your organization. So while "total revenues above €100M" is very measurable and might be determined in an instant, it is also totally arbitrary—which means that customers are more inclined to negotiate and try to pressure you on the distinction. If you have picked a nonarbitrarily determined principle such as "registered as a non-domestic tax entity," then the argument stops.

Note that this goes for both internal and external discussions: there should never be any discussion externally with a customer about which side of a fence they belong on, and you should never have a discussion internally within your sales or product team about where a customer belongs. Or, at least, these discussions should be so rare in reality that they never create any friction.

A poor example of fencing might be startups vs. corporates or digitally advanced vs. not advanced. If you can't determine it definitely in about ten seconds, then it's probably ill-defined.

Stable: Your fencing should be set up so that customers don't go from one side of a fence to another—or if they jump, it should be extremely rare and usually a once-in-a-lifetime move, such as a company switching from on-prem to cloud or a government organization reclassifying as a self-governing NGO. An example here might be classifying according to size, such as "small, medium, large" as companies can shift from one category to the next and back again.

It's the discreetness and stability of fences that make them different from what you might call *marketing segmentation*. They are not the same thing.

Marketing segmentation is an optimization component of your acquisition model. It's figuring out what sales process to apply to customers of the likely dollar value across various channels, etc. Part of that is fitting various customer attributes (such as size, geography, sector, past purchase history, etc.) into an overall statistical model to guide decision-making and behavior.

That has value, especially as a tool to allocate marketing spend and sales costs. But marketing segmentation is a broader tool than fencing, and it should be able to create sub-categories of customers and optimize these sub-categories at a much more granular level (e.g., on a regional basis, on past purchases, on marketing, or sales channels). It should also be much more dynamic and change on an ongoing basis to allow for optimal marketing and sales spend—something you don't want for your overall fencing level, which should be more stable across time.

Fair: Part of the power of fencing is that it allows you to operate in the market with several product and pricing models. This becomes much easier if the different customers will accept this as fair, as opposed to not.

If you sell edtech software to both individual professors and universities on two distinctly different product tracks and pricing models, this is likely to be unproblematic—a professor doesn't expect to buy the same product as an institution and vice versa. But if you sell, say, crop-optimization software to industrial farming conglomerates and price it based on their ability to attract subsidies from government bodies like the EU, while selling the same product cheaper to small farms, then perhaps open knowledge of this pricing scheme will get you into trouble.

Real considerations of ethics aside, the perception of fairness is often in the eye of the beholder and should be considered. The rule of thumb is that all your customers should be willing to buy even though they know about all your pricing, because they likely will sooner or later.

Obvious: If the fencing you are considering feels contrived, forced, or requires more than thirty seconds of explanation, then it's probably not a good one. Partly because your customers won't get it immediately but also because all your internal processes will have to align across these fencing lines all the way from engineering, through product, sales, marketing, and finance. Fencing is basically a proposition about how your market is structured, and if that isn't based in reality, then it's going to be difficult to organize around it.

The rule here is simple: Fence if it feels obvious. If it doesn't, don't.

Valuable: Finally, fencing has to pay off. If it doesn't bring you value through either higher pricing, more sales volume, or easier, less-costly sales, then you probably shouldn't do it (unless it serves some very well-defined future strategic goal).

The rule of thumb is that each additional fence you create should add 30 percent of CLTV/CAC (e.g., going from 5.0x to 6.5x) as compared to not having that fence in place. So if you can acquire 10 customers worth a total of $50,000 for $10,000 without fences, then fencing into two distinct fences should allow you to either lower that acquisition cost to $7,700 ($10K/130 percent) or up the CLTV to $65,000 ($50K*130 percent)—or some combination thereof.

Add 30 percent for each fence—and not as an average but as a threshold for each fence. So if your first fence, from, say, laboratories to food vs. pharma, adds 200 percent by suddenly unlocking a massive CAC decrease on food labs and a massive price upside on pharma labs, then that's great. But if you then consider adding another fence of "non-FDA-regulated laboratories" to the list to also acquire customers with less stringent compliance needs that might still buy your services, then this new structure should probably outperform the basic food vs. pharma with +30 percent on a CLTV/CAC basis to be worthwhile to you.

The exact percentage is size-dependent. If you are a $100M ARR company, you're probably happy with a 10 percent increase when you add another fence, but the basic principle here is that a fence should feel like a "big win" and not like you're just tuning the engine. You can do that elsewhere in your pricing model without adding the complexity of carving out a distinct customer group to serve with a specialized product and pricing scheme.

FENCES I'VE USED MORE THAN ONCE

1. **Vertical:** for example, defense vs. aerospace vs. automobile or, maybe, restaurants vs. manufacturing, etc. This is not always clearly definable, depending on where your technology fits in this space, but sometimes it is.

2. **Company type (subvertical):** for example, insurance companies vs. banks vs. pension funds, if you sell to financial institutions. Or food vs. pharma. Or, if you sell logistics software, perhaps warehouses vs. couriers is the right one for you. It can be hard to fence properly within a subvertical, but it might make sense and be straightforward in your case.

3. **Distribution chain:** for example, original equipment manufacturer (OEM) vs. distributor vs. equipment owner for an IoT solution that follows a piece of hardware through a value chain. Or maybe brand owner vs. shipping company vs. shipping broker if you sell software to handle import/export customs for retail goods, etc. This can be particularly powerful if you wish to incentivize one fence as a distributor to help you acquire customers in another fence, such as selling cheaply to OEMs to get access to equipment owners at scale.

4. **B2X:** B2B vs. B2C vs. B2Government.

5. **Sector:** public vs. civic vs. private sector.

6. **Cloud platform:** on-prem vs. cloud, sometimes also distinguished as private cloud vs. multi-tenant.

7. **Regulatory category:** for example, systemically critical banks vs. nonsystemically critical ones.

8. **Core systems:** for example, based on CRM (Salesforce, HubSpot, etc.) vs. based on ERP systems (SAP, Oracle, etc.).

A FEW EXAMPLES OF FENCES THAT ARE UNLIKELY TO WORK

- **Size:** small vs. medium vs. large.
- **Footprint:** national vs. multinational customers.
- **Arbitrary axis:** for example, technologically advanced vs. not-advanced customers (this is much better used as an organizing principle when laddering, as we will see in the following section).

Remember, a fence should make your life easier, not harder. Don't do it unless you feel like something clicks, a lot of product and pricing questions are easier to answer, and you are confident you can get a big win in the market.

JOBS TO BE DONE

Top-down packaging is essentially how most SaaS businesses approach their packaging. They try to create packages that revolve around a particular theme, use case, or technology.

Here is an example packaging draft from a large enterprise SaaS provider selling data analytics software to monitor and manage large logistics installations, such as the machinery that postal services use to sort mail.

The software provides value by reducing maintenance costs and stoppages, improving operational efficiency, and increasing the ability of management to plan for the future by recommending capital expenditures, reworking shift schedules, and so on.

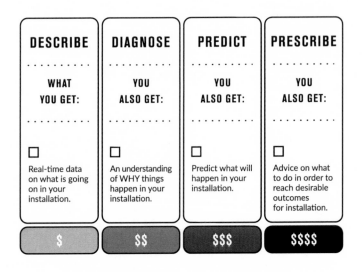

Figure 21: Sketch of a tiered packaging model from a customer workshop.

I call this a product ladder because the packaging shows a particular theory about who the customers are and how their use will rise over time.

A ladder runs on some axis—in this case, the axis is technological sophistication. Going from left to right, this packaging runs on an axis from simple to advanced. The thinking is that this software's customers will have a certain level of technological sophistication and readiness to adopt it. Therefore, they will start with a simple purchase that delivers a little value. When this works and they are happy, our sales reps can then upsell them to the next tier, thus progressing them through the different tiers of our product.

An expansion sale has been made.

The product team of this SaaS business built their packaging along a classic AI and machine-learning track. That starts with compiling data and describing it, then understanding why that data is as it is, before moving on to predicting what will likely happen in the future via machine learning. Finally, the team used this to run scenarios based on goal outcomes to start prescribing actions.

That makes sense from a development standpoint, as this is likely how the product was created. First, we create the necessary technology to simply collect the data. Then, we show it to the user. Next, we start analyzing. And so on. Each new stage in the development roadmap is "added to the right" and becomes a new advanced tier.

It's a simple process and perfect except for one tiny flaw: it doesn't work.

THE "JOBS TO BE DONE" THEORY

To work commercially, a product package should have its own source of demand. Or, put simply, your customers should be looking to buy this already. The best theory I've found to power this insight is the theory of "jobs to be done."[8]

A job is not the same as a problem. There are lots of problems whose solutions would provide tons of value to society (and to the people and organizations involved) that will never work commercially. The reason why they won't work commercially is that people don't perceive the problems that they solve as a job that they need to have done.

Let's look at an example of that. I once counseled a startup that tried to solve the problem of university students feeling disconnected and lacking meaning in their lives. The numbers it could

---

8 The concept and theory of jobs to be done was created by the late Prof. Clayton Christensen of Harvard Business School. I highly recommend googling "jobs to be done" to get the fast introduction, as well as buying his book *Competing Against Luck*, where he lays out the concept.

put on how much wasteful cost was created in higher education due to poor mental health were sobering. To tackle that problem, the startup created an app that would facilitate meaningful conversations between students. It had demonstrated that students who tried this would experience higher degrees of life satisfaction, better social connection, lower dropout rates, lower rates of suicide, and so on.

So big problem. Solution delivered. Value to the user? Maybe even your life! This should be easy to sell, right? No. At least not to students. They'd never buy this. They buy beers, books, smartphones, Spotify subscriptions, and so on—but not conversation apps.

Because even though they have a problem, they are not looking for a way to spend money directly solving it. It's not a job for them in the sense that they are actively searching for a solution or have an intention to get it done or solved.

So there is no intentionality, no direction, and no existing source of action that you can tap into and present your product as an alternative solution. And that intentionality is an absolutely necessary component of what we call "demand" for a product or service.

The customer has to have some idea of an "end state" they want to arrive at—not just a situation they don't want to be in. So while students don't want to feel disconnected, they don't have a clear idea of where they want to go. Therefore, there is no intentionality, no direction, and no demand. They need to want to go from A to B. Just "not-being-at-A" is not enough.

It turns out that to have an effective call to action, the action has to be already there for you to call.

Let's take an almost opposite example. I met an entrepreneur once who had created a platform called HomeBob, where you could subscribe to have your windows cleaned. He said it was the easiest business he had ever built because demand for window cleaning was so clearly expressed in the market. He simply had to buy the AdWords for "window cleaning X" (with X being the zip code served), and he would instantly get 40 percent of the window cleaning market for that area (as it turns out, window cleaners aren't very good at digital marketing). Then he just turned around and sold that customer to a local window cleaner for 30 percent less, arguing that he had already secured the work and would handle the billing, guarantee prompt payment, etc.

He told me, "I just had to hold my cup out—the water was already running," which is a great metaphor for what happens when you really get a job done for your customer. Demand is already there. Just hold your cup out.

ONE JOB FOR EVERY PACKAGE—ONE PACKAGE FOR EVERY JOB

The reason the tiered packaging model of the data analytics SaaS mentioned earlier doesn't work is that "describe" is not a job. It's a tool. I might use it to solve some job internally, but the packaging isn't telling me what job that is.

The same with diagnose, predict, and prescribe. All tools. If your product team sends packaging like this to the market, you are relying on your sales reps to explain to the customers how they can use it to solve their jobs: "So with Predict you will be able to create alerts on XYZ machine to reduce maintenance cost and downtime."

This is the core issue with the traditional good-better-best approach used to create the three-tiered SaaS packaging that you find everywhere in the form of basic, advanced, enterprise tiers or silver, gold, platinum, etc. It focuses on the functionality of your product, essentially spreading it out over three tiers. If you are lucky, the best tier is actually focused on a job the customer is looking to get done. But, more often than not, it just confuses the message and sells inadequate *good* versions of your solution to customers who really ought to buy *best*.

Here is the alternative: one job for every package.

Every package should have a clearly defined problem that it solves, with clear and present demand from customers to solve that problem. Every feature and service you have that helps solve that particular problem gets into that package—even if that means putting your new, shiny advanced feature into your most basic package.

Let's get back to the large enterprise SaaS provider and take a look at the jobs it is actually trying to solve for its customers. When I asked the product team, they unanimously agreed that the primary problem they were trying to help their customers solve was predictive maintenance. A large logistics installation, such as the system that moves mail inside a large postal facility, costs millions to build and even more to maintain and operate. If it shuts down for any reason, the cost per minute is staggering. So maintenance is a constant concern, which—because it's expensive—has to be weighed against its cost because logistics companies run on pretty tight margins. It is, essentially, a game of chicken. Maintain too little and take a huge hit from unplanned downtime; maintain too much and whatever margin you had is severely compromised.

So data analytics software that could tell exactly where to spend limited maintenance resources optimally was in high demand among customers, which is why the SaaS provider had developed the solution in the first place. Maintenance was definitely a job.

The real money, however, wasn't in maintenance but in operations. Getting a large logistics system like a huge e-commerce pick-and-pack facility or an airport luggage system to run more efficiently would be a huge cost saver.

Finally, management could also use the system to pull reports and potentially model the effect of extensions to the installation, such as adding more gates to an airport.

The product team saw the three primary use cases within their customers' organizations and tried to map their product roadmap of describe-diagnose-predict-prescribe across them, especially as they were technically only at the "diagnose" level and had to build from there. Simplified, this is how they viewed their product:

	Describe	Diagnose	Predict	Prescribe
Maintenance				
Operations				
Management				

Figure 22: Mapping out the packaging against the internal users within the customers' organization.

Each of their original product packages would provide a tool that the customer could then use to solve a problem within each of the identified problem areas.

The better way to do this would be to repackage the product around the identified jobs to be done, like this:

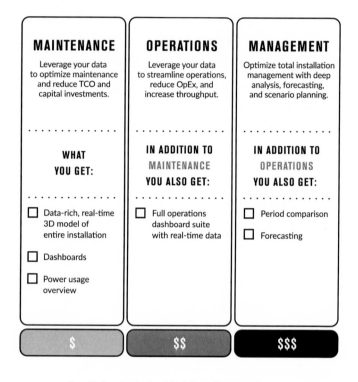

Figure 23: Reworked tiered model that aligns with the internal use cases and budgets of the customer's organization.

When you flip the packaging to reflect your customers' jobs to be done, instead of the capabilities of your solution, several good things happen immediately.

First, your customer instantly understands what she is buying. There might be some investigation and debate about how your product solves the job in terms of what features it provides (more on this later), but at least the package clearly communicates its intention. Which, incidentally, is perfectly aligned with your customer's intention. You want maintenance? We want you to have it. You just hold your cup out.

Second, you can actually price these packages because the customer's job to be done has a clear value associated with it. A logistics facility already knows what it spends on maintenance and what unplanned downtime cost last year. It knows what it spends on operational costs before adding in amortization and depreciation, and it knows what ROI it is expecting from its CapEx investments and how much a 1 percent increase would be worth. Whatever price you put on your individual packages, they will be immediately compared to these already-known economics, which is a good thing because that's where the value is to your customer.

Third, packaging that is driven by jobs to be done is just easier to sell. Not only because your customer gets what you're selling and can clearly connect it to their own economics, but also because it clearly shows that you—the solution provider—know what the job is! Customers, for some strange reason, trust you more if they sense that you know who they are, what they care about, and what they're trying to get done. This, of course, applies to marketing as well.

It all translates into shorter sales cycles, less discounting, and—to a lesser extent—reduced churn, which, in combination, has a tremendous impact on your CLTV/CAC ratio. It's not uncommon to see a 20 percent reduction in CAC and a similar increase in ARPA due to less discounting, just as a consequence of a jobs-to-be-done structured repackaging. This catapults your CLTV/CAC to 1.5x its previous level (as 1/1 becomes 1.2/0.8).

The real value in jobs-to-be-done centered packaging, however, is the internal effect it has on your entire organization, as it centers all your efforts around an outcome for your customers. Previously, your product team would create a diagnose package and tell your sales team that this could be used for all sorts of good things. Sales would then take the product to the customers, try to understand what job they needed doing, and explain how the product could help do that. They would then carry feedback from the customers to the product team in the form of feature requests. "The customers want a dashboard to show them workflows. Oh, and anomaly detection is a huge problem too. A lot of value there. And this customer over here won't buy until we have a power usage overview." And so on.

Because all this feedback returns home to the product team in an unstructured format as individual features and not as core jobs, the product team runs the risk of simply developing more and more tools. They may hodge-podge them together in good-better-best style packaging that the sales team can then lay at the feet of the market, hoping the customers can find something that's actually useful.

If, instead, the organization is clear on the jobs it is trying to get done for customers, the entire line of communication from the product team through sales and on to customers clears up. Product can issue a maintenance package and ask Sales to talk to customers about how well it does the job of maintenance. This feedback is a much more useful way to guide a product roadmap—simply because it's much more direct and contains much less noise from other jobs.

TIERS, MODULES, AND ADD-ONS

CHOICE ARCHITECTURE

Once you are clear on what packages you have for sale in your product model, you have to decide how each of them can be selected through a structure of tiers, modules, or add-ons. This is what is called a product's choice architecture.

First, you should determine if parts of your product are a mandatory purchase. It is almost always the case that there is some basic software that simply must be delivered for any of your product to make sense. Tear the roof off the wagon here and call this the base package.

If you only have two packages—A and B—and one of them is a mandatory base package, then the whole choice architecture discussion is a moot point as the only choice you are giving your customers is whether to add the non-base package or not. Whether you call it a second tier, an add-on, or a separate module is purely semantic. With A as your base, you have only two options: A or AB.

The problem arises when you have three packages or more: A, B, and C. Now, you have four potential settings: A, AB, AC, and ABC.

The joys of permutations and combinations can produce pretty staggering numbers of possible choice architectures with only a handful of product packages, especially if you have interdependencies in your product such as "if you choose B, you can't choose C, and if you now choose F, you have to also choose G." That kind of logic is a necessary evil if you structure large-scale enterprise solutions across several layers of APIs, third-party integrations, and business models.

However, this is partly the point: the mix simplifies the choice architecture. If we tier packages ABCD, we're now down to four choices—A, AB, ABC, and ABCD—instead of the potential eight. This, of course, is also much easier from a product management perspective.

For annual contract values (ACVs) below about $25K a year,

you should be able to tier almost everything. In some cases, ACVs in the multiple six figures can be based solely on tiered models.

The decision about whether to make something a module or an add-on should be driven mostly by whether you, from a technical perspective, can deliver the package at all stages of your product architecture and whether you, from a customer success perspective, want to do so. If the answer is yes, and you are fine if the customer buys this after the purchase of the base package, then this is a module. If the answer is no, then make the package only available to purchase once the customer has already bought some other level of product, and then it's an add-on.

If your sales team wants to modularize everything—i.e., have no predetermined interdependencies on how the solution is sold—you ought to ask yourself if you've captured your customers' "jobs to be done" properly or if you are simply selling tools.

Don't capitulate by creating the "uni-product," where you simply give all possible features to the customers in a single package and then slug a price out in negotiations. This is fine for pushing your minimum viable product (MVP)[9] into the market with the first run of customers, but not beyond that.

So if you can, tier your product choice architecture. Otherwise, let technical and delivery constraints drive the choice architecture across modules and add-ons.

SERVICES

Services have several key functions for the growth of your SaaS business. The first thing to notice is that services, by and large,

---

9 MVP refers to the earliest version of a product that has just enough features to be usable.

are peripheral to your core functionality. They are not the product itself, but they help customers get value out of the product.

Onboarding and migration services help them get started. Support, training, and professional services help them get value out of the day-to-day use of the product. Same with bespoke development, configuration, managed services, and so on. None of them "are" the product, but all of them help the customer access or multiply the value of the functional features in the product.

Because of this, there is a good argument not to monetize services and simply give them away. That can sometimes be the right approach, but it probably isn't as you grow.

Take a look at this overview, adapted from Brian Stolle from Wildcat Venture Partners (data sourced from companies' S-1 and 10-Q filings, board reports, and management interviews):

COMPANY	@ MVT (APPROX, $5M)	@ GROWTH ($20M–50M)	@ IPO	TODAY (2018 NUMBERS)	SERVICE COST/ALL COST
Workday (HR app)	40.00%	34.00%	34.00%	16.50%	14.40%
Marketo (Marketing app)	n/a	8.60%	9.70%	12.60%	11.20%
Coupa (Spend management app)	25.00%	15.30%	11.80%	13.10%	10.80%
Mulesoft (App integration)	n/a	15.90%	18.60%	20.50%	16.40%
Rally (DevOps app)	35.50%	18.70%	15.30%	20.40%	10.00%
ServiceNow (Service app)	n/a	8.30%	17.00%	8.40%	7.90%
NetSuite (ERP app)	n/a	n/a	27.20%	28.40%	20.40%
Apptio (IT management app)	n/a	26.50%	18.40%	15.90%	13.60%
Cloudera (Data Management app)	n/a	33.50%	23.30%	18.10%	11.50%
Zuora (Billing app)	45%	33.30%	28.30%	28.20%	22.80%
Average	36.40%	21.60%	20.40%	18.20%	13.90%

Figure 24: Service revenue is a key part of B2B SaaS as it adds incremental revenue to each customer. Adapted from an original version by Brian Stolle from Wildcat Venture Partners.

This data is from ten B2B SaaS companies from the US. Across time, from about $5M ARR all the way up to their IPO and beyond, you can see how they all eventually included services into their revenue mix.

Services are easy to monetize because there is such an obvious cost element on your side when delivering them. Customers are (mostly) reasonable and know that somebody has to pay the salaries of the people who do the servicing. Usually, they realize that one way or another, they are that somebody.

My general rule of thumb is this: be quite generous with services, especially the ones around onboarding and adoption. If you charge for them, do so mainly to communicate the value delivered. As you grow, add real value-adding services, such as managed services. Realize that for your very largest customers, services are going to be a reasonably large part of your total revenue from them, as they will have a lot of bargaining power to reduce the prices of your core software offering.

In any case, from a choice architecture perspective, most services should function as either base offerings—i.e., something the customer simply has to buy—or as an add-on that is purely optional as long as any other product is purchased.

IMPLICIT FENCING

Sometimes, if you have quite distinct use cases but not many potential jobs within each one, it's better to use a tiered product model for price discrimination across customer segments. This is called *implicit fencing*, and it creates a structure where every potential customer has one—and only one—package they should buy, and you have plans to upsell them to a more expensive package.

	FREE	PRESENTATIONS	DEVELOPERS	DESIGNERS	INTEGRATION PARTNER

FREE

200,000 icons on Creative Commons licenses — free to use

Creative Commons — free forever

☐ Use any of the 200K free icons — forever.

☐ Creative Commons license

☐ 1 user

FREE

PRESENTATIONS

Use for internal purposes or in mass-produced sales material

World's largest icon database

☐ Use any free icon (+3 mo)

☐ No license expiration

☐ Easy-to-use icon editor

☐ 1 user

$19.99/month

DEVELOPERS

Use for commercial purposes in your own product(s)

Everything in previous plan plus:

☐ Multiple file formats (svg, gif, pdf, xyz)

☐ Multiple sizes

☐ Save your favorites

☐ Up to 5 users

$39.99/month

DESIGNERS

Use icons in your work to your customers freely

Everything in previous plan plus:

☐ License allows free editing

☐ Even more file formats (gwt, etc.)

☐ Priority support

☐ Unlimited users

$79.00/month

INTEGRATION PARTNER

Integrate the world's largest icon catalog in your product

☐ High-speed API

☐ Account manager

☐ Custom onboarding

☐ Icon development on demand

Call us

Most popular!

10 icons | 25 icons | 50 icons | 100 icons | 500 icons | 1,000 icons | Unlimited icons

Figure 25: Mock-up packaging for iconfinder.com. As it turned out, they only needed to add "roll over icon credits"—a commercial feature—to transform results.

The packaging mock-up shows a discarded draft for Iconfinder. com, the world's largest icon repository. The packaging tries to clearly separate different types of users and price them differently. The features—such as commercial use rights—are used to ensure that designers don't buy the cheaper "presentation" pack, which is meant for corporate warriors who just want icons to spice up their slide decks.

Using your tiered model to price discriminate across customer types is essentially an implicit form of fencing executed at the feature level. It's good when your product isn't deep enough to do several jobs for a given customer but is outstanding at solving one job for several distinct types of customers, each needing slightly different features to do the job for them.

Consequently, it tries to monetize each customer type immediately without a subsequent plan for expansion revenue through product upgrades. Expansion revenue here comes only via increased usage, which isn't always easy or possible to create (one can only use so many icons in a PowerPoint presentation, after all).

EXPANSION: PRODUCT LADDERS, AXES, AND STORIES

TIERED MODEL FOR LAND AND EXPAND

The other use of a tiered model is to design it to power a land-and-expand strategy, where customers first buy the smallest tier and then upgrade to more expensive tiers over time, thus promoting expansion revenue through product upgrades. This is what I call "laddering," as the product is designed in stages to take the customer from A to B.

Importantly, I don't think a land-and-expand strategy really works in SaaS unless you base it on a tiered product model with a laddered structure in it. You might get there with modules and add-ons too, but these are inferior to a well-designed tiered model.

Conversely—and also importantly—I've seen quite a few land-and-expand strategies fail because they were based on either "uni-packaging," where there was no next product to upsell to customers, or an implicit fencing model, where each tier was designed to capture and keep a specific customer segment and not move them up a ladder. The only expansion possibility that leaves is increasing some pricing metric, like "number of users," which isn't always practically possible, nor desirable, for the customer.

So if you are aiming for a solid land-and-expand strategy in your SaaS business, with a +120 percent net dollar retention being the benchmark for "good," you should design your product model around a laddered structure.

That is the model illustrated in Figure 25 with the logistics SaaS company. Here the design intention is to get the customers to sign up for maintenance and then get them to upgrade to operations and management over time.

POINT OF FIRST DEMAND

One key question to get right in a laddered, tiered model is what step to put at the beginning of the ladder. In Figure 24 from the logistics SaaS provider, the sequence of the ladder was maintenance-operations-management, but a reasonable question is, of course, why not the other way around? At least in good-better-best, it's clear what order to put the tiers in.

The truth is that there can be several ways to solve this with no one correct answer. However, there are a few design concepts that can be useful when sequencing a product ladder as the foundation for a land-and-expand strategy and optimal expansion revenue.

The simple answer is that whichever of your potential jobs is easiest to sell goes at the bottom of the ladder. I call this the "point of first demand," which is simply the job around which you have the most articulated and accessible demand stream to tap into. If you put your cup out, under which of your job packages would it fill the fastest? For the logistics SaaS company, this is "predictive maintenance," which has a lot of expressed demand in the market. For HomeBob, this was window cleaning even though it also provided gardening services, cleaning your gutters, etc.

I sometimes ask my clients, if they were running out of cash and had to scale sales fast, and I told them they could only buy one AdWord, which would it be?

There can, of course, also be technical reasons why one package must structurally come before another. This is the case with "maintenance," where the analytics and data collection needed here is also a prerequisite to being able to perform the job that is done in "operations." You simply can't deliver them technically in reverse order. That, however, is not the case for HomeBob. There is no technical reason why window cleaning precedes gutter cleaning or gardening—there is simply just more demand for it.

Once you have the bottom step of the ladder—your "land" package—you have to determine the second tier (i.e., the one you want your customers to upgrade to next). This is surprisingly hard. One reason is that you, as a SaaS team, can see the entire product journey and have an intimate understanding of all the compounding benefits of adopting your product suite more completely. For that reason, I see a tendency to try to make the second tier what the customer *ought* to want to buy—rather than focusing on what the customer actually wants to buy. Usually, the customer wins that argument.

Ask yourself the following question: "By solving this first job for my customer, which job emerges next as the most pressing to solve?" Often, this second job is one that it is now possible to do because of something you solved in the first package.

When my windows are clean, I can now take a look out at my garden and see that my trees and hedge need trimming. Oh, and maybe I want to solve the job of having to order window cleaning all the time, so perhaps you could sell me a subscription to this? This is exactly how HomeBob drives expansion sales.

Or, when I've optimized the maintenance work of my logistics facility, have zero downtime, and have access to all this beautiful predictive data from my installation, maybe it's time to take a look at how much efficiency I can squeeze out of this?

The reverse of this wouldn't make sense. If my system breaks down to a complete stop without warning, I'm focused on keeping the damn thing running when I need it to, not edging out another 2 percent operational efficiency. In other words, there is a clear hierarchy between the two concerns.

Note that the question "By solving this first job, which job now emerges as the most pressing to solve?" forces you to think of each step of the ladder as something the customer transitions into from the previous step. If you want your customers to upgrade from "advanced" to "enterprise" in your product ladder, you better have designed "enterprise" to appear to be the perfect solution to whatever job your "advanced" customer is trying to get done.

If you are simply trying to design "advanced" for one particular customer segment and "enterprise" for another, you are not creating a product ladder. You are using implicit fencing just like Iconfinder did. There's no harm in that; you have a very solid foundation for monetizing your customers. Just don't expect product upgrades to contribute to your net-dollar retention.

If it's a ladder, design for the transitions and the journey. If it's implicit fencing, design for the underlying segments. Choose.

ESTABLISHING AN AXIS FOR TIERED PRODUCT PACKAGES

I sometimes think of a ladder of tiered product packages as if they are running along some common axis or theme. For HomeBob, that axis runs from need-to-have, frequent tasks that all house owners must do on occasion (window cleaning) to nice-to-have, infrequent tasks that are only relevant to some homeowners (like the removal or pruning of trees). For the logistics SaaS company, it moves along the economics of their customers' installation, where management first buys the installation with CapEx, after which the operational teams use it to run the logistics facility, supported by the maintenance teams.

Mistakes and errors are most visible at the end, near maintenance, even though any issue might, of course, be due to poor management decision-making. An example would be underestimating the necessary size of a new installation, which cascades into an unrealistically high-operational efficiency requirement. In turn, that makes any errors in maintenance much more costly. So we start solving the job of maintenance because it appears as the point of first demand, and then we use our product ladder to move backward along the value chain in the organization.

Could we have come up with another axis? What about laddering the product across an axis that went from small, single-location installations to customers with multiple locations? Wouldn't that promote a land-and-expand strategy, where customers try it out at one location and then increase usage by adopting it across all locations later?

Or what about an axis that takes technical sophistication and the availability of data from the installation into account? The first tier creates value from basic data extracted from old installations, followed by steps up the ladder to full utilization of all possible data sources from high-tech, modern installations.

Sure, whatever works best. The axis or theme of the ladder in a tiered model is a conceptualization that you use to understand your market and to which you fit your product. It's not something that is just out there in the world waiting for you to discover.

It's not something like a continent or a mountain range, which exists independently as a geographical feature. It's more like searching for "places where people speak English." If you are looking for a formally correct definition, you are in the wrong place.

When we are doing top-down packaging, we're in design-thinking mode. We're trying to create something that works, not something that's "right."

ILL-POSED PROBLEMS AND INTELLIGENT DESIGN SOLUTIONS

If you are an engineer—or have the mind of one—you might consider this whole business of jobs to be done, product ladders and themes, and axes to be pure nonsense. You might object that it's an ill-posed question, which is impossible to answer in any correct sense, and you are right.

From the pile of data that is the world of problems your customers have, plus all the features you have or could build, there is no one true "product" that you can create. No "right" solution. Not even an "optimal" or "best" one (because how would you know?).

You are trying to get to product-market fit. I suggest you consider "fit" in the evolutionary sense of the word, as in "survival of the fittest." There is no correct organism, only ones that manage to survive and thrive in a given environment. Period.

Swap your engineer's brain for a biologist's one. It'll help you survive.

PRODUCT LADDERS AS STORIES

A crucial aspect of your product ladder is that it has to function as a story that your sales rep can tell your customer. You start here, then you go there, and then you end up here.

Is this a journey the customer wants to take? Maybe, even, is excited to take? "What? You can clean my windows *and* my gutters, prune my trees, mow my lawn, and take away garden waste? So I can live in my beautiful house without all that hassle? That sounds awesome, but I'll start with just the windows today to see if you are someone I'd like to hire for all those jobs." A land-and-expand strategy works exponentially better if the customer actually wants to move all the way up the product ladder on day one but just needs time to do so.

Same with the logistics SaaS: if the customer can see from day one how the solution might help them improve everything from maintenance to CapEx investments in new facilities, they are more likely to buy.

This point is crucial: the high end of the product ladder helps sell the low end—the starting point. I might not be ready for "management" because I need to solve "maintenance" right now, but I like the prospect that your product can take me there when I'm ready.

The higher your ACV, the more crucial this point becomes—and I'd say it becomes a key point around $50,000 ACV. If you are selling true, solution-level enterprise software, the customer is likely expecting to be a customer for five-plus years (just as you are in your CLTV predictions). So they need to know they can evolve with your solution.

That is one of the key reasons your product team and your sales team need to align on the product packaging and the story of the ladder of jobs to be done. If there is no good story to tell that you have all agreed on, your sales reps will simply invent other stories to tell. They will listen to where the customer wants to go and what five-plus-year journey they are on, and they'll try and match that to your product.

After one or two years of trying to scale these types of sales, you'll have a team of high-level sales reps who each have their uniquely justified opinions about why the customers are buying and what direction the product roadmap should go in. If your product team is weak, they will try to accommodate all the various feature requests that come through. Customer success will serve an ever-larger product across widely different applications with customers who are expecting widely different things from you. That problem is most common in sales-led SaaS companies that have a good initial product they want to blitzscale.

The reverse version of that is a product-led organization that misses the crucial distinction between a "job" and a "problem." Not ensuring that the sales team is reporting back that they have a very compelling story to tell and is just "holding its cup out," the product team seals the door and drives a roadmap for which there is no real demand.

Note that they are not sealing the door to the customers—they can be talking to customers every day. They can co-create and map out use cases from here to infinity. They are sealing the door to the sales team, and that is a mistake.

Your head of product and your head of sales should have an extremely strong shared understanding of what you are trying to achieve as a business. If they are not regularly high-fiving each other, you have a problem.

TOP-DOWN PACKAGING—SUMMARY

So in summary, here is the top-down approach to product packaging:

- **Fence your customers.** If you are trying to serve fundamentally different customer groups, don't try to fit one product packaging to all. Split it up and design for each individually. The rule of thumb is that fencing should make your life easier, not harder.

- **Implicit fencing or product ladder.** Inside a given top-level fence, decide if you want to create a product ladder that promotes upselling over time, or if you simply want to monetize segments using implicit, feature-driven, second-level fencing.

- **Each package has to solve a job, not a problem.** Define what jobs your product can solve for customers. Recognize that a problem is not necessarily a job. For every tier, you should be able to put your cup out in the market and have it filled with preexisting demand. This is true for both a ladder and implicit fencing.

- **Start with the point of first demand.** If you are creating a ladder, make it as easy for yourself as possible to land that first tier with a customer. This is where you should really feel your product-market fit. Ask yourself, "What if I could buy only one AdWord?"

- **Organize your product ladder on an axis.** Create a progression up your product ladder that makes sense in each transition from one step to the next. Ask yourself, "By solving this job for my customer, what job is now emerging as the primary one?"

- **Have Product and Sales align on the story.** Is the product ladder telling your customers a compelling story? Do they want to "go all the way?" Is your head of Product high-fiving your head of Sales?

Now that we've covered the product, it's time to turn to pricing models. We do that in Chapter 4, which explains why, contrary to popular belief, complexity is a virtue when it comes to pricing.

--- FOUR ---

PRICING MODEL

THE CULT OF SIMPLE PRICING

The one thing I hear most often from SaaS executives when I'm designing their new pricing is they would like it to be simple and easy to understand.

I always ask them, "How much are you willing to pay for that?"

Tongue-in-cheek, of course. Because for some reason, simplicity in pricing is this universally agreed-upon design principle that shalt not be questioned. It is seen as the one necessary pricing component of SaaS success and blitz growth.

There are zero instances of profitable, publicly traded B2B SaaS businesses with simple pricing structures, but there's this unwavering belief that simple pricing equals growth, despite all the contrary evidence in the world. That's why I call it "the Simplicity Cult of SaaS Pricing."

Simplicity is highly dependent on what you sell to whom. When you are bringing your MVP to the market, you should probably aim for something simple, but for anything more complex than that, you should not. What you really want is for your pricing to be easy to sell, and that is not the same thing as making it simple.

You have to balance the two core elements of what a pricing model is to get this right:

1. A pricing model is the mechanism by which what your customer buys determines what they pay.

2. A pricing model structures how that price is different from customer to customer.

For example, imagine you have a product that you want to charge per user the customer signs on, like a piece of productivity software that is good for small teams or something similar. You determine that a price of thirty bucks per user per month is about right. So one user equals $30, and five users equal $150.

This model simply charges a fixed amount per user, which creates a linear pricing slope, like this:

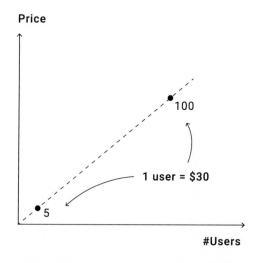

Figure 26: If one user is $30, then one hundred users is $3,000. Using just one pricing metric creates a simple, linear relationship between price and unit cost for the customer.

Pros: simplicity. It takes one question and about one second to calculate pricing for any customer.

Cons: Can you really charge $3,000/month for a customer with 100 users? Or will this potential game-changing customer expect a substantial discount on the #User-based pricing, like paying $10 per user?

So this basic model is really good at determining what each customer will pay, but it's not very good at discriminating between different types of customers and offering each a price you believe they will accept. That's the problem with simple pricing: it over-values the first element of what a pricing model is—calculating the price for the individual customer—and undervalues the second element—the discrimination between different customers.

So you could get creative and slap on a flat fee to your model so the price is now $500 + $30 per user, creating this scenario:

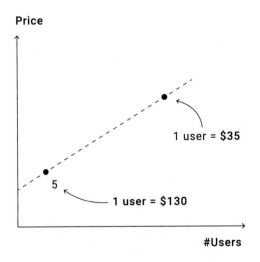

Figure 27: Same as above, except now a $100 flat fee is added. While a small piece of complexity is added with the flat fee, this also creates a de facto volume discount as cost per user goes down for the customer if more users are bought.

Now, the price for your five-user customer is \$500 + (5*\$30) = \$650, which is \$130 per user. Whereas for your 100-user customer, the price is \$500 + (100*\$30) = \$3,500, which is \$35 per user. In this case, the pricing model is now substantially more expensive for smaller customers on a per-user basis but almost the same for larger clients.

It is also *less simple*.

What you get for adding in the complexity of a flat fee is that this second model is very likely to be more attractive to your larger customer than the first one. Why? Because your model is seemingly already taking their size into account. They are, after all, already getting a 73 percent discount per user compared to the five-user customer. So if you are mainly interested in larger customers, this complexity works in your favor.

Willingness to pay is affected by what that hundred-user customer can see the five-user customer is paying, even though in principle, they should be totally unrelated. I hear economists with torches and pitchforks approaching. Or is it the cultists?

THE NINE BUILDING BLOCKS OF SAAS PRICING ARCHITECTURE

Complexity is a tool you use to price discriminate between different customers. The rule of thumb is that the larger the ACV, the more complexity you need.

Let's go over the complexity toolbox you have available to you in terms of the elements or building blocks you can use to structure your pricing model:

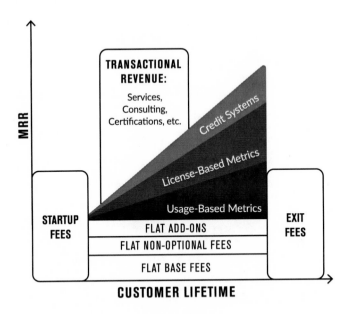

Figure 28: The nine building blocks of SaaS revenue: three types of nonrecurring transactional fees, three types of flat recurring fees, and three types of metric-based fees. While the X and Y axis are not super consistent (e.g., transactional fees are not "MRR" as the Y axis would have you believe), I've kept this illustration as is since I first drew it on a whiteboard five years ago in a workshop. It is by far the most popular, shared, and phone-photographed of all my illustrations.

There are three basic elements, each of which has three sub-elements.

TRANSACTIONAL NONRECURRING FEES

This is any charge that you put on your customer that isn't perpetual or recurring in nature but is, instead, transactional. "I give you A, you pay me X." Done. With such an arrangement, there is no relationship tomorrow. There is no ongoing delivery and no ongoing payment.

In a SaaS context, there are three sub-elements to this, which are organized before, during, and after the core as-a-service relationship with a customer:

- **Setup fees:** Any and all fees you charge as part of onboarding the customer. This can be a fixed charge for getting the solution up and running, add-ons for additional training, or a price per hour in a time-and-material format. (I once helped an insurtech company build into their model a one-off $500K upfront charge for "participation in their intellectual property." Customers paid it.)

- **Ad-hoc one-offs:** All the transactional fees you charge the customer during their lifetime with you. This can include professional services, additional training, pulling reports, etc.

- **Exit fees:** All charges you put on the customer as parting gifts. These can be consulting hours in off-boarding, charges for record keeping in compliance with regulatory requirements, the annulment of some form of credits in their account, etc.

FLAT FEES

These are charges that do not change or fluctuate depending on a metric. The $500 fee from the previous example is a flat charge. The $30 per user is not. There is an ongoing relationship and delivery involved, hence the charge is also recurring. There are three basic sub-elements to flat fees, ordered according to how dependent they are upon customer choice:

- **Flat base fees:** These are fees that occur as a consequence of a customer's core product choice. They are used to: 1) set minimum charges, effectively closing your product to the smallest customers, and 2) lower the incline of the pricing slope from small to large customers (e.g., the $299/month for a Shopify "Advanced" shop is a basic subscription fee).

- **Flat add-on fees:** These are flat, recurring add-ons that you charge your customer as the consequence of some product choice but do not feel are suitable to be tied to a metric. This can be a good monetization model for small, auxiliary add-ons you don't want to discuss or negotiate too much with customers (e.g., the $89/month for Shopify's "POS Pro" add-on), but it can also be a good tool to push costs onto a customer (e.g., $150K/year for the extended hours of your enterprise support hotline). These product choices can be tied to a metric too, of course, such as $150K for extended hours plus $5 for every support ticket.

- **Flat non-optional fees:** Recurring flat fees that are not the result of some particular customer choice but are added regardless of what your customer chooses to buy. These fees do not fluctuate by any metric. If you are selling large ACV enterprise software to banks, you can—so I've heard—add a flat "ISO 27701" fee annually, essentially monetizing your compliance efforts around the General Data Protection Regulation (GDPR), irrespective of what the bank actually bought from you as part of your product model's choice architecture. In contrast to flat add-ons, such fees are not dependent on what the customer buys—just simply that they buy anything. Integrations, co-pay for data feeds, compliance, and security are good candidates for flat fees.

METRIC-BASED FEES

These are perpetually recurring charges that are dependent on some metric. The classic example is a price-per-user, but it can be anything that is structured as a "price-per-X," where "X" is somehow delivered on a perpetual basis without the need for a new customer purchase decision.

The rest of this chapter gives lots more details about metrics. However, from a pricing-architecture point of view, metric-based fees are structured just as flat fees with three basic sub-elements, ordered based on how dependent they are upon customer choice:

- **Metric-based license fees:** A license is a right to use something; the classic SaaS example being a user license. This means that the customer decides the volume to be purchased before using it, effectively limiting their own usage. That creates a stable and predictable recurring charge and is well suited for solutions that have relatively stable and predictable usage patterns, such as if you are pricing #StoreLocations or #VirtualServers and the like. You can combine several metric-based fees to the same basic subscription, such as both $30/user and $200/team.

- **Consumption and usage-based metrics:** Consumption-based metrics are all metrics that are charged based on the behavior of your customer (or your customers' customers), but where the volume or amount purchased is not determined prior to the charge but rather post-fact as a measurement of interaction with your solution. For example, #Users is determined in advance as a license-based metric, but #MonthlyActiveUsers is determined after the fact and charged accordingly. Consumption-based metrics have the advantage that the customer only pays for what they use. Typical consumption-based metrics include #Storage, #APICalls, #SupportTickets, and #PercentOfRevenue-Generated. Consumption-based metrics are good at getting your customers to cover costs (e.g., #APICallSeconds from Microsoft's Azure Purview) and good at capturing excess value generated (e.g., #PercentOfRevenue from Hungry.com), but they have the disadvantage—to both your customers and you—that they can be unpredictable. Customers tend to care greatly about the predictability and variance of consumption-based metrics, as well as who is doing the consumption. Is it the customers' (cost responsible) management, the (reckless and cost insensitive) employees,' or, God forbid, the (totally unpredictable) customers' own customers? You and your funding partners might care about how to really predict consumption-based ARR. Is it even recurring?

- **Credit-based metrics:** Credit systems are a hybrid model between licenses and consumption-based metrics. Credits are a right to consume or use something at a later stage, but the usage is estimated and paid for upfront. The most well-known B2C credit-based model is Audible.com, which has a subscription that gives you one or more credits every month. The credits accrue in your account until you decide to spend them by downloading audiobooks. Credit systems are especially great if you have high seasonal variance where usage comes in fits and bursts. They do add a level of complexity to your pricing model, but they can create predictability for both you and your customer (and remember, complexity can be good).

Here is my estimate on how I see the SaaS revenue mix evolve across fee types for different ACVs:

SAAS REVENUE MIX	TRANSACTIONAL FEES	FLAT FEES	METRIC-BASED FEES
ACV <$25K	0-10%	20-40%	50-70%
ACV <$25-100K	10-20%	10-25%	55-80%
ACV >$100K	15-25%	5-15%	60-80%

Figure 29: This is a rough guideline and starting point. Your particular case is almost certain to have its own best revenue mix. But the core point remains: certain types of revenue seem easier to execute at certain ACVs.

Importantly, the type of metric-based fees shifts as the ACV goes up. For low ACVs, expect a large proportion of metric-based revenue from base subscription fees. For large ACVs, expect a relatively large proportion to be based on consumption-based metrics.

Could your B2B SaaS business be completely different from that? Sure, these are just my general estimations of what pricing architecture tends to support what levels of ACV.

Regardless, your primary takeaway should be that metrics are king, making up the majority of your revenue at all ACVs and all stages of your growth journey. Having done pricing design for more than one hundred SaaS companies, from pre-revenue to multi-billion ARR, and ACVs from sub-$1,000 to +$10M, I have never come across a case where, after a bit of discussion, it wasn't clear that the best way to monetize a customer—while at the same time designing for proper price discrimination between customers—was to use metric-based pricing at the core.

The only thing that sometimes comes close is for on-prem installations or installations in private clouds, but this is mainly because measuring the metric can be difficult in such cases—not because metric-based pricing isn't the best choice. For example, I once helped a Scandinavian software house design pricing for an on-prem SaaS product that had +50 percent of all defense intelligence agencies in the world as customers. Getting these customers to share usage data was a little bit difficult. In the end, we settled on a simple model with flat fees across feature functionality plus #User-based pricing, creating a cap in the software on how many users could be created. Not perfect, but better than a flat fee alone.

I usually say that if you find the right pricing metric, you are 80 percent done with your pricing model. The rest is just balancing.

PRICING METRICS: VIABILITY, VALUE, FAIRNESS, AND DENSITY

So what is a good pricing metric?

I use the following four parameters to evaluate pricing metrics:

1. Operational viability
2. Demand and value-chain position
3. Expectation to pay and fairness
4. Metric density and monetization

Once you understand these four parameters, you will never look at pricing metrics in the same way again.

OPERATIONAL VIABILITY

The first parameter is whether a pricing metric is practically usable. This usually comes down to a binary yes/no answer to the following two questions: 1) Can we measure it nonarbitrarily, and 2) can we execute our financial process to invoice based on this?

If you can't measure it, it isn't a metric. You might start out with a vague idea of having your chatbot software price per #SatisfiedCustomer, but until you have a very clear technical definition of that, which your customer will actually agree with, you are still at the drawing board.

This can get tricky as you sometimes think a metric is perfectly and obviously well-defined until you actually get to the end of a project and have to implement it. I once did a project for a large, multi-billion ARR fintech company that sold white-labeled trading platforms to banks. We charged per #MonthlyActiveUser. But do the users who are trying out empty demo accounts count here? Or what about someone who receives dividends into his account? Or what if one of his stop-loss trading rules activates and sells a stock for him? Or if he replies to an automated broker email but never actually logs into the platform? What if his legal guardian or designated portfolio manager logs in and performs trades on his behalf? What if this portfolio manager does bulk trading for hundreds of thousands of accounts? Are they then all active?

None of these individual questions are that hard to answer. But sometimes it happens that one of them actually hits a roadblock. Maybe there is a compliance issue in measuring this, or maybe your IT infrastructure needs to consolidate a tally on a quarterly basis that might then change some of these numbers retrospectively. This is not good news if you've invoiced customers based on the early numbers.

So while it sounds almost simplistic on the surface, you can only price based on something you can reliably and nonarbitrarily measure and present in a timely manner to the customer who has to pay for that measure.

DEMAND AND VALUE CHAIN POSITION

Take a look at the following price list from 2021.AI, which delivers the AI platform "Grace" primarily to banks and other financial institutions:

GRACE LICENSE*

CORE AI/ML PLATFORM		#MODELS IN PRODUCTION			
Users	Size	1–4	5–15	15+	Included Components
up to 8	Small	8,000	10,000	15,000	Github integration
up to 20	Medium	10,000	12,500	18,750	Small + Nifi
enterprise	Large	12,000	15,000	22,500	Medium + Hadoop/Spark
					*ex. Deployment & support fee

Figure 30: Pricing from 2021.ai. Real numbers not used. Pricing model uses two pricing metrics—#User and #ModelsInProduction—lined up in a matrix.

We have two pricing metrics at work here: #ModelsInProduction and #Users. The logic is that an AI model that is put into production generates value for the customer (as well as some cloud costs for 2021.AI), hence the customer should be willing to pay more as more models are put into production. In addition, the logic is that large banks have large AI departments and staff counts and, therefore, need more users. A large bank will get more value out of the same number of models on a net basis compared to a smaller bank.

This is the first intuition that most SaaS companies try and execute in their pricing models: to have metrics track value generated, based on the premise that higher value should equal higher willingness to pay, all else being equal.

Sounds perfectly reasonable. The only drawback is that it's a false premise. At least in some instances, which is enough to create major problems in your pricing model.

The problem is that even if a metric tracks value perfectly, that doesn't necessarily mean that there is demand for it; sometimes customers actually want to buy as little of it as possible!

Let's unpack the 2021.AI case to illustrate that. The first question I asked the management team was whether #ModelsInProduction had value for their customers? Yes. So far, so good. Did customers also actively want more AI models in production? Yes. That was sort of the point of buying the Grace platform in the first place for customers; they want to design and implement AI models to improve a broad range of business outcomes. In principle, more is better.

But when I asked the exact same two questions for the #User metric, the answers changed. Does the number of users have value to the customers? Yes. Okay. Still good. Do customers actively want more users? No. On the contrary, customers want as few users as necessary to create the models they want.

That is why 2021.AI had never once sold more than the minimum of eight users in its first sale to a customer. The sales conversation was always the same:

2021.AI: How many users do you want?

Bank: Well, how many do we need?

2021.AI: That depends—more users equal more value, after all!

Bank: Yeah, that makes sense. But I think we'll start with eight and then go from there.

2021.AI had tried to bypass this dynamic by reserving some premium features, like Spark, for larger #User purchases, effectively slapping on tiered packaging to the number of users purchased.

This created the issue that the customer still wanted to start with eight users but now felt they were being forced to pay for an "Enterprise" number of users, which in this case was defined as anything over twenty.

That creates the following situation:

GRACE LICENSE*

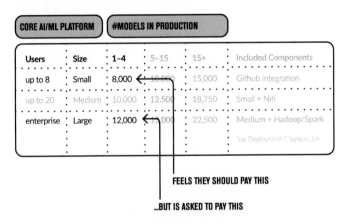

Figure 31: Absent an obvious, concrete value to compare price against the reference point for any price delivered by the 2021.ai pricing model becomes other price points in that same model. The customer asks themself a very local question: "Is the difference in price between scenarios A and B fair, considering the extra value I get?" Instead of asking overall, "Is this worth it?"

At that point, it doesn't matter if Grace is worth €12,000/month to the customer. I'd argue that nobody knows what an AI platform might be "worth" for a bank. All the customer cares about is that they feel the pricing model is forcing them to buy something they don't want. The customer's solution to that is to ask for a discount, and if your sales team is worth their salt, they will give it to them. Often, high use of discounts is a clear sign that you have an issue with your packaging or pricing.

Remember, nobody disagrees that #Users aren't highly correlated with value. Not even the customer! We need to unpack how a given metric "tracks" or "is equal to" value in order to understand why there is demand for #ModelsInProduction and not for #Users.

VALUE METRIC CHAIN

Imagine you are the customer bank and have decided you'd like to start using AI in your business. To get that job done, you'd probably start by placing the responsibility for AI development somewhere in the organization and giving that team the appropriate budget and executive blessings before sending them on their way. The new AI team would start to source data in the organization and come up with good business case ideas for AI models: better credit scoring of customers, churn predictions, and all the other things a bank might want to get done by the intelligent use of data.

The team would then start to build and test the models before deploying them in the business with the relevant departments that would need them. Finally—hopefully!—the models would work and improve the relevant business outcomes they were designed to affect.

Simplified, the AI value chain of the bank looks something like this:

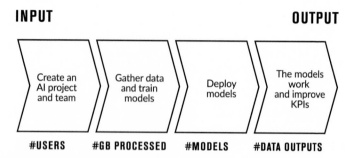

Figure 32: A simple value chain analysis of the 2021.ai case shows how #users and #models are placed at opposite ends of the value creation process—#users as an input and #models as a (near) output.

Critically, however, one end of the value chain is input while the other is output. One end is investment (also known as costs), and the other is return. Each step in the process is necessary for the next and—ultimately—for the value that is generated in the end.

If our software supports this value chain, we can decide where on the customer's value chain we would like to attach our pricing. If we attach it at the beginning, we can price per #User, monetizing the size of the team our customer deploys to run the AI project. We can attach it at Step 2, by monetizing the data that goes into the models or the infrastructure necessary to run them. This could be either #GBProcessed, #CPUSeconds, #VirtualCores, #Queries, or something similar. The idea would be more data equals larger bank equals higher price. In Step 3, we monetize the business cases themselves, charging them for the #AIModels they run on our platform. Finally, we can also, in Step 4, monetize the business outcomes by attaching our pricing to some form of final output, such as #CreditScores or #ChurnPredictions.

The customer will view our pricing metric differently depending on where in their value chain we decide to monetize and attach our pricing. If we attach at the input end, we're viewed as an increase in the necessary investment to get the value chain started. If we attach at the output end, we're viewed as a value-sharing partner, especially if we also support the earlier parts of the value chain. So while #Users are close to the output end of the value chain of a product like Slack, or other productivity and communications software, that metric is certainly not for a product like Grace.

Don't get this wrong: if you price Grace using the metric #Users, the bank will accept it. They know they will have to make investments to get returns and that #Users are a necessary part of generating value. But they will minimize the investment, especially as they are testing their new value chain and your effect on it. They will start with eight users, and only when the value chain has run its course and the AI models eventually generate value will they consider buying more users. This is your expansion sales cycle—the time it takes your customer to increase their purchase with you.

If you attach your pricing at the beginning of your customer's value chain, your expansion sales cycle takes as long as it takes the customer to execute their value chain. That might be something like two years for a development project in a bank.

What would happen if you simply made users free? The bank would now add users indiscriminately. These users would find more data sources, come up with more use cases for AI models, and would, in comparison, deploy more AI models into the bank at a faster rate.

Because you haven't constricted investment into the beginning of the value chain, you increase your chances that the customer invests more heavily, both speeding up the turnover of the value chain and increasing the volume pushed through it.

So instead of five models after twenty-four months, you might get six models after twenty-two months. That might not sound like a lot, but it is actually a +30 percent increase in the efficiency of the customer's value chain. Over a ten-plus year customer relationship, that is a huge difference in outcome for your customer and for you, because as a primary enabler of that outcome, you should be able to increase revenue on that customer dramatically.

A good principle for designing pricing in SaaS is for your value chain to be aligned and intertwined with that of your customer: you support them at the beginning, and throughout, with your product and share value at the end through pricing.

Value chains are like rainbows: the gold is at the end.

FAIRNESS

So should 2021.AI just price the Grace platform according to some form of #DataOutputs and share in the value generated by the AI models in their banking customers' organizations? Put another way, should you always just pick the pricing metric that is closest to the end of your customers' value chain? Unfortunately, no.

Let's use an example to illustrate. Imagine you're at home one evening when a water pipe bursts in your kitchen. With water everywhere, you scramble to turn off the main water line. Once done, you search for a plumber on Google and call one. Forty-five minutes later, the plumber arrives. When you let him in, he says, "You're lucky I could find parking in the street just outside—it's not always easy in this neighborhood." Then, just before he walks into your home, he notices your nice floor, takes off his dirty shoes, and puts them outside in the hallway.

Then he walks into your kitchen, fixes your pipes, leaves, and sends you an invoice the next day with the following three items on it:

- Two hours of emergency plumbing plus spare parts: $220.00
- Parking: $3.52
- Shoe fee: $10.00

If you're like most people, you're fine with the first two but have what we in the business call a "low willingness to pay" for the ten dollar shoe fee. But why? A craftsman who cares about all aspects of his service is surely valuable to you, and you'd likely have rated something like the taking off of his shoes and being mindful of your home as "very important" if you were asked to score it on a one-to-five scale.

It's because value isn't the only determining factor in willingness to pay. Your customer has to have an *expectation to pay* as well. Value determines if they want what you have, but expectation to pay (ETP) determines if they think it's fair for you to get paid for it.

Introducing the "Price Perception Matrix of Expectation and Value:"

Value to Customer

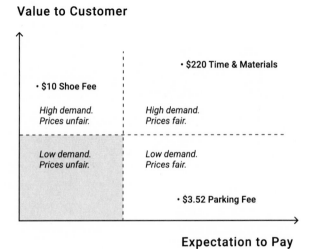

Figure 33: The combination of value and expectation to pay creates a quick overview of the likely performance of a pricing metric in a sales context.

Expectation to pay is determined by three things:

1. **Habit:** Is this how you're used to paying for something like this? Your financial advisor charges you a percentage of the assets you ask him to manage, your accountant charges by the hour, and every SaaS solution in the world could charge on a #User basis simply because we are so used to paying per user for software.

2. **Cost transparency:** You have a high expectancy to cover the costs associated with what you buy—if you understand them. You understand that plumbers have to pay for the parking in the street and that your accountant probably needs a salary. The average customer of B2B SaaS will also accept covering infrastructure costs, such as #API-Calls, cloud costs, etc.

3. **Similarity:** Especially when it comes to a new domain or purchase, we tend to accept it as fair if we're introduced to a pricing model that is very similar to something we already know. Netflix priced movie rentals per month on the basis that their service was similar to a newspaper subscription. Nowadays, you can sell pizza on a subscription because we're so used to the model.

So while the parking fee has a very high degree of cost transparency, implicitly communicating that its purpose is to cover your plumber's cost of delivery and not to generate profits for him, it scores lower on expectation to pay overall as you might not have paid for parking with a craftsman before. Conversely, you would be surprised if you *didn't* have to pay for time and materials, and that category also conveys implied costs for the craftsman, such as spare parts, wages, etc.

The shoe fee, in contrast, has very low expectation to pay. It clearly cost the plumber nothing to take off his shoes. You are used to people being polite and considerate without paying for it, and there is no immediate similar reference case you can use to understand the fee.

Let's plug in the potential pricing metrics of 2021.AI into the Price Perception Matrix:

Value to Customer

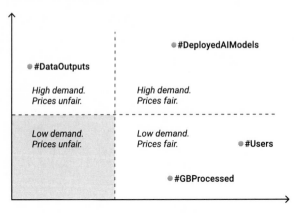

Figure 34: Plotting in the four example pricing metrics from the 2021.ai value chain analysis shows that while #DataOutputs has the highest perception of value—being at the end of the value chain—it is unlikely that customers are expecting to be priced on this metric, likely creating a sense of unfairness if #DataOutputs is used as the lead pricing metric.

As you can see, #DataOutputs has the highest value—consistent with its position at the end of the customer's value chain. Customers had, however, a very low expectation to pay. Why? Because they felt the data outputs were closely connected to the ideas and business insights that designed the model—something they contributed themselves with only little input from 2021.AI. Also, they are not used to paying per #CreditScore or other output and have no immediate point of reference where this is the norm. Finally, they feel it is not related to the costs of running the Grace platform. As a result, the banking customers felt that output-based pricing would simply be unfair.

Note that this is an estimation exercise, not a precise measurement. Usually, I simply ask everyone in Product, Sales, Marketing, etc. to score each feature or pricing metric on both value and ETP from the perspective of a given customer segment on a scale of one to ten. Afterward, I ask them why they scored as they did to gather insights. Only very rarely does this result deviate too much from the results you'd get from surveying the actual customers.

Conversely, #Users and #GBProcessed had relatively high ETP scores but low value scores. They have high degrees of habit and cost transparency connected to them, respectively.

Just to repeat the point: that is a result of the particular circumstances of 2021.AI, their Grace platform, and the customers they sell to. These exact same metrics might work completely differently for another product sold to other customers. That is exactly why you can't just walk into the market and copy the pricing of a SaaS company you admire. Just because HubSpot does something doesn't mean it will work for you, just as you shouldn't follow the training regimen of an Olympic skier if you are competing in the discus.

For simple pricing models and lower ACVs, it is by far the best approach to find a "fair value pricing metric" that hits that sweet spot combination of value and expectation to pay for your product. You will then enjoy customers who have demand for and want to increase that metric in and of itself while at the same time perceiving it as fair to pay for it.

However, for larger ACVs, which usually have more complex product structures and larger customers, a fair value metric might not do it on its own.

METRIC DENSITY

Some pricing metrics will count a unit of value that is not only very well defined and obviously at the end of the customer's value chain but also very uniform. In the sense that one unit of the metric is very alike any other unit that the metric measures.

The best example of this is software that charges a percent of revenue or money flow—like payment providers. One dollar is identical to the next dollar. So if Stripe charges me 2.95 percent of the transaction in fees of two payments of $100 each, I've not only paid the same in each transaction, I also feel like I've gotten the completely same value out of them.

The #Dollar pricing metric is, therefore, extremely dense.

Contrast that to another example: Lyfegen is a Swiss insurtech company that handles repayment flows between insurance and pharma companies. Repayments are a specific form of discount that pharma companies give in the form of repaying parts of the original price at a later point in time, depending on how well a drug or treatment performs in a clinical setting.

Lyfegen has #Patients as their pricing metric. One of their largest customers—a major Swiss insurance company—has about one million patients each year, and Lyfegen could earn them about twenty dollars in optimized repayments. So the pricing math seems easy: just charge $10 a patient, and both parties make $10 million. Right?

No, because while the average value of a patient is twenty dollars, that covers an extremely wide range. A few patients who receive expensive, experimental treatments are worth $1 million or more, while the vast majority of patients are worth zero dollars as there is no repayment optimization to be gained from them, something that isn't knowable before Lyfegen has processed them through their platform. To the insurance customer, this creates a situation where they feel they would overpay for 95 percent of their patients if Lyfegen charged ten dollars per patient.

This creates very real friction in Lyfegen's sales process as potential customers push the company hard to reduce the ten dollars to one dollar or two dollars. Even then, Lyfegen would face a scenario where the insurance company would likely try to sort its patient flow and only process those patients who have a higher likelihood of actual repayment value. That would result in even lower customer monetization for Lyfegen and—critically—also a lower value for the insurance company, which would now feel it has to run a presorting process to get a fair deal from Lyfegen.

The #Patients pricing metric has very low density.

VALUE CURVES

Low density of a pricing metric is created by one of two scenarios, depending on how the value that it is tracking is distributed across the metric: fat-tailed bell curves and power law distributions.

Power law distributed value is the most extreme of these two cases, and it is what is troubling Lyfegen in the previous example. Power law distributed value happens when most of the value of a given metric is lodged in a few units of that value.

Here is a sketch of Lyfegen's value distribution across the #Patients metric:

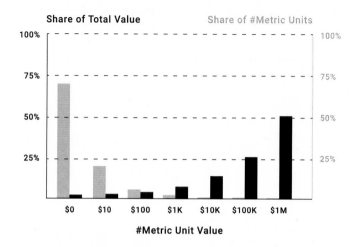

Figure 35: If value is distributed in a power law fashion across individual units of the pricing metric, the average value is far larger than the mean value, which is what the customer is likely to focus on because it represents the most frequent occurrence.

Power law distributed value within a pricing metric makes it hard to monetize a high share of the value being generated and tracked within that metric because almost any price point is going to be perceived as too high when considering most of the actual instances of the metric.

The underlying mechanism is that while you are focused on the fairness of the pricing at the metric level, your customer tends to be focused on the fairness of the pricing at the unit level.

If we pay ten dollars per patient, is that generally a good idea? No, 75 percent of patients are worth zero dollars. But the average patient value is twenty dollars!

Deadlock.

The customer usually reacts in two ways, as in the Lyfegen case. First, they argue the price is too high and push for discounts. Your sales reps will try hard to defend the narrative of the average value of the metric unit while the customer will be focused on formulating a response about the irrationality of paying anything above the median value. Then, after the sale, the customer will try to "game" your pricing, and if at all possible will create a selection or sorting mechanism to not give you all the volume of that #Metric.

Everyone loses here. Product adoption is essentially stunted; you don't get to process the full volume of units; and monetization potential is low.

The rule of thumb is this: the median value of your pricing metric should be as close to the average value as possible.

That, however, brings us to the other potentially problematic value curve: the fat-tailed bell curve:

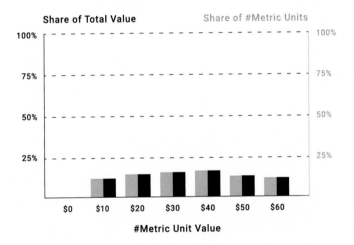

Figure 36: If value across metric units is distributed in a bell curve fashion it now becomes important how "fat" the tails are. Again the governing psychological principle is that customers do not want to overpay locally on a unit basis.

In the example in the graph, the average value is very close to the median value—about thirty-five dollars, but that still leaves a very large portion of the total #Metric units below that value. It's a bell-curve distribution with "fat tails" (if you want more visual representations, google images of "negative kurtosis").

In principle, a fat-tailed distribution of value should create the same issues as a power law distributed value metric: many unit instances are going to be below your price point, so customers should argue for lower prices and—post-sale—try to only send through those units that are clearly worth more than your price point. In reality, however, the issue is rarely as critical—simply because the mismatch isn't as extreme.

If you have a low-density pricing metric in place, you can do one of two things: 1) find another metric altogether, or 2) try to define your current metric to more closely fit the customer's value.

Take Slack as an example: it prices per active user, not per user. #User is a low-density pricing metric for Slack as a large proportion of its users would get a login from work but never actually use the software (especially in the beginning before Slack had its breakthrough). The value discrepancy for the buying company between an employee actively using Slack and one that isn't is, well, all of the value of Slack.

That is solved by simply selecting the subset of #Users who are #ActiveUsers and only pricing them. You can argue that one active user of Slack is more valuable than another, but that is likely to be both a small and an irrelevant issue, since a large proportion of the value comes from them both being active together.

#ActiveUser is also farther back in Slack's value chain, meaning there should be more in-built demand for this refined metric, but don't confuse the two. Metric density governs monetization and value extraction, while value-chain position governs demand. High demand for a unit is useless if willingness to pay for that unit is very low and fraught with conflicting psychology and vice versa.

Think of it this way: A customer has high demand for M&M's, but he values red ones three times as much as brown ones—even though he likes those too. If your pricing metric is #M&M's, you capture that high demand but at a low density. If you refine to #RedM&M's, bingo.

PRICE PERCEPTION MATRIX

I usually visualize all four parameters inside the Price Perception Matrix like this:

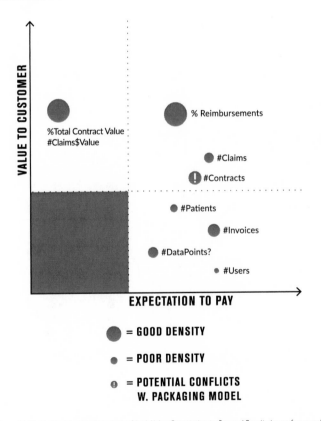

Figure 37: Illustration of a sketch analysis of both Value, Expectation-to-Pay, and Density in one framework. Use this framework to guide thinking along design paths and don't try and turn it into exact science.

Value-chain position and ETP are the two axes, while density is visualized as the size of the circle. Operational viability is simply marked with an "!" inside the circle if there is an operational conflict.

There are several ways to gauge and measure "value" and "expectation to pay," as well as metric density (see the sidebar on this one). Usually, the core team who has to decide on pricing can get the job done with a simple one-to-five Likert scale for value, fairness, and density, while a few yes/no type questions will sort out the operational viability.

Here is a customer example of how that can look:

#	Metric	Clearly Definable	Measurable	Execution Mechanism	Demand /Value	Fairness/ Expectation to Pay	Density
1	Users	Yes	Yes	License Based (built-in usage threshold)	1 No clear demand	4	4
2	Monthly Active Users	No	No	License Based (built-in usage threshold)	3	5 Fair/High Expectation to Pay	5 High density/ low or zero variance in unity value
3	Systems	Yes	Yes	License Based (built-in usage threshold)	5 Clear Demand	5 Fair/High Expectation to Pay	1 Low density/ high variance in unity value
4	Echelongs	No	No	License Based (built-in usage threshold)	3	1 Unfair/Low expectation to pay	3
5	Instances	Yes	Yes	License Based (built-in usage threshold)	4	3	3
6	Locations	Yes	Yes	License Based (built-in usage threshold)	3	2	3

Figure 38: Spreadsheet model of the four parameters of pricing metrics: Operational Viability, Value, Expectation-to-Pay, and Density. Gives an overview of the viability and performance in a sales context of all your potential pricing metrics.

Ultimately, of course, it's your customers who decide on the value and their expectation to pay (see Chapter 7 on Validation for this one), but your team will usually have a pretty good initial idea.

QUANTIFYING DENSITY

The density of a pricing metric can be quantified as follows: median value divided by average value multiplied by the share of metric units that has a value at or above the median value.

So median/average * percent units above or at the media.

In the Lyfegen example, that creates the following: 0/20 * 100% = [infinitely small].

In the fat-tailed, bell-curve example, we get something like the following: $35/$35 * 50% = 0.5.

Stripe has perfect 1.0 metric density with the following formula: $1/$1 * 100% = 1.0. They have a perfectly uniform distribution of value, with one dollar of transactional value for a customer being identical to any other one dollar of transactional value. While no single dollar unit is above the median value, every single dollar is at that value. There is no distribution. A dollar is simply a dollar here.

GENERALLY, THIS PATTERN HOLDS TRUE FOR METRIC DENSITY

- Density 0-0.25: poor monetization of value created, with several critical issues in both the sales process and product adoption. Generally, only suitable for short-term market testing of demand for the core product offering.

- Density 0.25-0.50: subpar monetization with some issues in the sales process and product adoption, often with heavy discounting and sales cycles extended by negotiation. Can be workable long term if you have very strong packaging that discriminates well between customers. A better pricing metric would, however, likely unlock very significant value.

· Density 0.50–0.75: strong monetization with only minor issues. You can get by with subpar packaging (but shouldn't). Unless obviously stronger alternative pricing metrics are possible, you should probably stick with this one.

· Density 0.75–1.0: excellent monetization. Sales and adoption processes are easy to make smooth. Can outperform outright counterproductive packaging.

CHOOSING THE METRICS

Unless you have a clear winner that just scores all fives on your internal ranking and is easy to implement operationally, you have to use common sense.

That does happen, of course. Stripe's model that charges you a percentage of the transaction is a perfect example of an "all fives" pricing metric: customers have extremely high demand for getting the transactions through and would never limit the amount to get rid of Stripe's fee. They have a high expectation to pay, as all credit cards and payment models through the history of time have charged in this way, plus the fact that Stripe probably incurs some marginal cost of processing each transaction. Finally, the density of one dollar is perfect. There is zero variance.

But most likely, you will have to make trade-offs. If you have a packaging model that allows it, covering several modules, add-ons, etc., you can use different pricing metrics for different packages as they apply to functionality and the job to be done. For example, if you have a payment module, charging a percentage of payments for that module makes sense while your core, tiered structure might be charged on a #User-based license model.

This is also a matter of managing the right level of complexity and balancing it against the monetization potential of your pricing architecture. Ultimately, it has to be communicable in a sales situation.

I usually advise focusing on a high value, high expectation to pay core metric to drive sales and expansion. Density is more about monetization, which you can probably solve in other ways by diversifying your product model, adding service revenue to larger clients, and so on.

At least with these four parameters, you now have a clear understanding of how metrics work, and why they sometimes don't.

REVENUE MIX: MONETIZING COMPLEXITY

Even if you have a good pricing metric, it will run into trouble with the larger customers in your market for the simple reason that those "whales" will know that the volume of business they bring to you is important and will want to test what kind of purchasing power they have got as a result.

So we get an outcome like this:

$ per #Unit

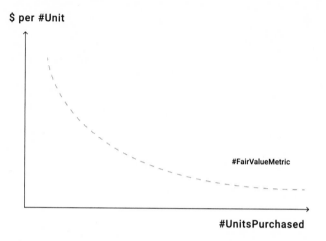

#FairValueMetric

#UnitsPurchased

Figure 39: The discount curve. In almost all markets, larger volumes produce lower unit prices simply because customers leverage the fact that you attain scale at larger volumes.

This means that a customer who buys 1,000 units of your metric (e.g., #Users, #Models, #WidgetTokens) very likely isn't paying 100x as much as a customer who is buying only ten units. Either because you set it up that way to begin with or because the whale negotiated a discount. How much less per unit depends on the market you're in, the product you're offering, and so on, but almost universally, volume is a key driver of lower unit prices.

One solution is to just slug it out in negotiations. You price $1,000 per unit per year, so if the customer wants to buy 1,000 units, then your opening bid is a cool $1 million a year, and anything less is a tug-of-war across the negotiation table. I've seen startups turn into high-growth scaleups because they had a co-founder or a VP of sales who was just very talented when it came to commercial negotiations. It just doesn't scale very well. More often than not, I find $5M ARR companies that are built on a long trail of legacy customers, each one being "the whale" when they were first closed, but many of which today are now considered small fish in comparison to the deals the SaaS company wants to target. Just by cleaning up the massive volume discounts that were given during past sales negotiations, we can often 2x–5x their ARR (not a typo).

If you want to consistently defend pricing during negotiations with whales, you need to add complexity to your pricing structure. You can't depend on Sales to just "discount less."

The good thing about whales—which we'll spend the entire next chapter on—is that they are used to paying for far more things than small fish and have a much deeper understanding of costs. We can use this to create pricing models that look something like this:

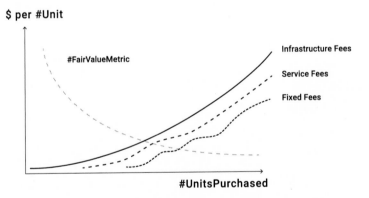

Figure 40: For individual large–"Whale"–customers, the pressure to lower prices on your core pricing metric can be offset by introducing other revenue sources and monetizing other parts of your value proposition.

For large ACVs, the revenue mix comes from more sources. The unit price of your main pricing metric has been lowered due to negotiation pressure from the size of the customer. But you have added other sources. The fixed fee might increase as the customer chooses the "Enterprise" package with all the features that it will need. Services are now bought as add-ons, and the limits for free usage of certain infrastructure intended for smaller customers have been surpassed.

Take a look at the two sample models below:

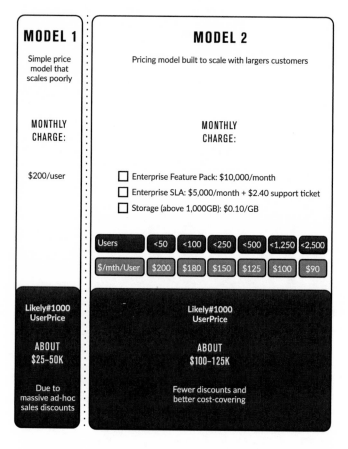

Figure 41: Sketch example of how to create packaging and pricing to defend against price pressure of large customers. Revenue mix is introduced by monetizing the offering more broadly and the discount curve on the core pricing metric is controlled via an up-front tranched pricing.

In Model 1, we simply charge $200/user/month. That is simple and straightforward, but it fails to show the whale what it gets for being a whale. So the 1,000-user customer who—remember—really likes your product, realizes you are not used to dealing with customers of this size, etc., and gently reminds you that surely there must be another price more suited for this situation.

And the problem is you will agree with that. You don't expect everyone to pay that $200/user. You *know* it doesn't scale. So build a pricing model that you and your sales team actually want to defend. A pricing model that shows the whale what it gets for being a whale and what it doesn't get.

Model 2 charges a flat fee for access to the "Enterprise Feature Pack," adds another $5,000 flat for an increase in the service-level agreement (SLA), and then adds two additional pricing metrics: one for support tickets ($2.40/#Ticket) and one for storage ($0.10/#GB).

This is just to illustrate that you can add different elements to your pricing architecture as long as each new element makes sense to the customer you are trying to sell it to. In Figure 41, our #User price is our "fair value metric." It communicates that we are bringing value, have a business to run, and we'd like to get paid for it. But the #SupportTicket and #GBStored are simply additional metrics we might insert into a pricing model as they communicate that the customers' usage of our product creates costs for us. Consequently, the customer will have a high expectation to pay, which we tap into by simply asking him to.

Importantly, Model 2 also shows the whale—at the same time—both what the small fish will pay for, say, 40 users *and* what the even-bigger whale will pay for 2,000 users. Both are important. The base unit price of $200 communicates the value and shows what discount the whale is already getting; in this instance, they would pay $100/user. Fifty percent discount? Not bad. But it also shows what volume the whale needs to show up with to unlock even-bigger discounts. In this instance, the cutoff is $90/user at

1,250 users or above. That makes it very hard for the whale to argue they should get a $50/user price.

Just imagine for a second that you are the customer of this software. How differently would you approach negotiations when presented with these two different models? Model 1 gives you no clue as to what price you should pay, given that you are a whale, so your instinct is to just push. Hard. Model 2, on the other hand, not only shows you what you get for being a whale but also, to some extent, shows you what the software vendor is getting. Or rather, that there are certain cost elements in running the service desk and storing data that are simply intrinsic to you doing business together that—presumably—the software vendor does not get to keep.

That essentially means that you are carving out a portion of your pricing and labeling it "nonnegotiable." This sets up your sales team for success. If the pricing model clearly communicates that a portion of the charge you are asking your customer to pay is simply covering your costs, then those parts will be left alone in 90 percent of negotiations. That means you will only negotiate discounts on what's left. So if we imagine that we can charge around $5,000 each for support tickets and storage, then together with the SLA charge and the flat feature charge, we've put a base of around $25,000 into our bid. The 1,000 users times $100 then comes on top and is likely going to be the main target of discounts in negotiations. That's fine because you are now starting this negotiation from a distinctly different vantage point: the whale knows its size has already been taken into account in the initial quote, taking the price from $200/user to $100/user.

So unless you're delusional in what you're asking for your product, the whale will now seek far smaller discounts: 10–30 percent rather than 75–95 percent.

In conclusion, simple is good only if you are selling primarily to one type and size of customer. If you cover a range of differences in your market across type, need, and size of customer, you need to add complexity to your pricing architecture to structure the sales properly.

It is especially important to realize that while a "fair value metric" is a brilliant tool to both communicate value and charge different prices to different customers, it is also the primary target of price negotiations. As the customers get bigger, this exacerbates, and you need to support your fair-value metric with some boring "parking-fee-type" charges to get the job done and defend your pricing in negotiations.

After all, you can't expect to catch a whale in a net made for small fish.

Next, in Chapter 5, we look at how understanding your customer's organization allows you to calculate appropriate charges for each part of their structure based on the principle "make everybody pay."

FIVE

WALLET STRUCTURING

ENTERPRISE SOFTWARE IS BOUGHT BY A COMMITTEE AND EACH MEMBER HAS HER OWN BUDGET

One of the key questions that I almost always ask my clients is, "Who buys your software?" By this, I don't mean the type of organization they sell to (e.g., "FMCG brands with a global presence") but the actual person who wants their software and decides if it's a good fit (e.g., "We usually sell to the global head of marketing").

However, in nearly every case, there are two to five other people sitting next to that primary stakeholder. If you are selling directly to the business line in your customer's organization, these auxiliary stakeholders can be the chief information officer or another key technical stakeholder, the chief compliance officer, the chief operating officer, the chief human resources officer, the head of procurement, the chief legal officer, and so forth. Your primary stakeholder—the person your sales rep has a relationship with and who is trying to get a job done by buying your software—is dependent on each of these supporting functions to buy your software, have it embedded into the organizational processes, and make it run properly. Hence, each of them has the power to block the sale.

I call this committee of buyers "the Wallet." Because—just like an actual wallet—the Wallet of an organization consists of various compartments, each with its own distinct function, some of which hold money.

The size of the Wallet you are dealing with depends on: 1) the size of the organization you are trying to sell to, and 2) the size of what you are selling. I find it usually looks something like this:

WALLET SIZE	Small customer	Big customer
Small ACV	1–2 stakeholders	1–2 stakeholders + maybe minor interest from 1–3 other companies
Large ACV	2–5 stakeholders	Task force reporting to 5–25 stakeholders

Figure 42: The customers' "wallet" is simply a metaphor for the group of stakeholders involved in purchasing the SaaS solution from you. Larger purchases and larger customers mean more stakeholders.

If you are selling a multimillion-a-year solution to a global organization, you can bet you are going to have to meet with *everyone*. The customer is likely to have an entire team whose job it is to purchase this solution from you (or your competitor). That team will then keep the various executives informed, pull them in and out of negotiations, etc. The sale itself is a project with Gantt charts, several stages of co-creation, bespoke development, and, finally, eventually, *maybe*, the signing of documents.

If you are selling a small solution of less than, say, $20–50K a year, this will fit into the budget of a single stakeholder. If the organization is small (such as one selling tools to a design agency), your buyer is likely to be the managing partner. If the organization is a little larger (such as one selling market analysis software to a regional office of a manufacturing company), you might talk with the regional head of marketing, who could be wing-manned by one other stakeholder, such as the chief of sales. She might pull in other functions (e.g., the technical department, HR), but that would be merely to inform the organization around her, not to gather consent. So in that case, the sales cycle should be relatively short and not involve too many other people. It is her budget and—because your software isn't an overarching solution that spans the organization—also her decision.

I don't find that this stakeholder situation can be bypassed, even if you sell directly to the CEO. The size of the solution trumps the seniority of the stakeholder you are dealing with. Senior executives of large organizations haven't got to where they are today by forcing things on their organizations.

Most B2B SaaS businesses that I work with recognize this situation of selling to a group of people, but they also, almost unanimously, see it as a negative. It drags out sales cycles as everyone needs to get heard. Plus, the scope of the solution can blow out of proportion because you need to fit it to the needs and desires of each part of the organization (e.g., Compliance wants a particular report or HR wants to train the Canadian office to use your solution too).

However, this situation also creates opportunities. If you understand it well and adapt your pricing structure to it correctly, the Wallet can be used to your distinct advantage. Because the customer's budget structure usually follows its organizational chart pretty closely, each of the stakeholders involved also has a budget.

So that gives you a budget structure onto which you can map your pricing structure.

PRICE EVERY BUDGET IN YOUR CUSTOMER'S ORGANIZATION

The rationale is simple: make everyone pay. That means that every stakeholder whose part of the organization your solution touches, and who participates in the committee that decides whether to buy it or not, should (or at least could) be asked to pick up part of the bill.

You do this by asking each stakeholder to pay for things that they are used to paying for. Compliance is used to paying for reports, audits, and security measures. IT is used to paying for storage, cloud computing, API calls, developer hours, and so forth. The COO of an industrial cleaning company is used to paying for staff, floor scrubbers, and leases on cars.

If we re-use the example of 2021.AI from the previous chapter, we can now redo the Price Perception Matrix from the viewpoint of each primary stakeholder to get something like this:

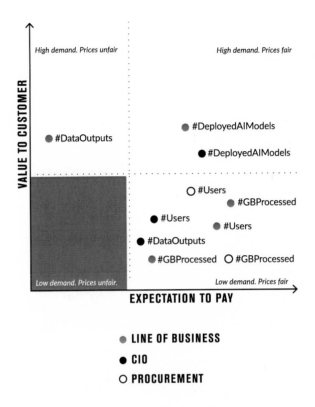

VALUE TO CUSTOMER

EXPECTATION TO PAY

High demand. Prices unfair

High demand. Prices fair

#DataOutputs

#DeployedAIModels

#DeployedAIModels

#Users

#GBProcessed

#Users

#Users

#DataOutputs

#GBProcessed   #GBProcessed

Low demand. Prices unfair.

Low demand. Prices fair

● LINE OF BUSINESS
● CIO
○ PROCUREMENT

Figure 43: The Value-Fairness matrix can now be further loaded with information by mapping each metric to a primary customer budget. At first glance this reveals how certain pricing metrics are viewed differently by different stakeholders.

This is simplified, but hopefully, the message is clear: considering the differences in value (demand) and expectation to pay (perception of fairness) from several viewpoints within your customer's organization can be an eye-opener.

In the example, we see, among other things, that #DataOutputs means something completely different to the business owner compared to the IT department. For IT, a data output is just another product in the portfolio of things they will be responsible for running. Unlike the business as a whole, they know there are quite a few costs associated with this, so the IT department is likely to want as few data outputs as necessary. On the other hand, both IT and procurement realize that #GBProcessed represents a cost to you as a vendor, and they are, consequently, prepared to cover that cost.

In fact, the unbundling—or spinning out—of IT costs is, in many cases, a great opportunity. For example, I once helped a European insurtech company, which made around $100M in ARR on less than thirty customers—all large insurance companies. Part of their solution was to store terabytes of data and documentation related to the claims the insurance companies were handling (e.g., X-rays, MRI scans), but with millions of claims that all had to be stored for decades due to compliance, this storage load added up. To a degree, in fact, where we could forecast that a new insurance company would start at an 80 percent margin and then, over about nine years, drop to zero percent, after which they would be loss-making. Not so scalable.

The answer to that problem was simply to ask the IT departments of these large insurers to co-pay for the solution, which had previously been loaded directly to the head of claims management. We raised prices about 50 percent, with zero churn, and secured high margins going forward without impacting the budget of our primary stakeholder.

The core principle, which is illustrated in the Pricing Perception Matrix is that your primary buyer is the one who pays for the value, while all the auxiliary buyers pay primarily because of expectation to pay. The main drivers for this are the perceptions of fairness and cost-covering. The organization you are selling to has a budget structure because it expects to pay for certain costs. Each of its individual budgets has its main stakeholder as a guardian who ensures that the budget is spent wisely.

So if you arrive to demo a piece of software that enables your customer to produce widgets much better and find that the head of widget production has pulled in the head of compliance, the chief information officer (CIO), and the HR partner, then hopefully, you'll leave something like the following pricing for them to consider:

Pricing for Widget SaaS Solution:

1. $5,000/month for core license + $1 per widget produced.

2. $5,000/month for regulatory compliance as per national widget regulations.

3. $7,220/month for cloud setup + $0.000001 per API call.

4. $1,200 per day of on-site staff training.

Each item lines up with something that each of these stakeholders already knows intimately. The head of widget production will, of course, pay the core license and your one dollar per widget. If that fits his unit economics, and he thinks it's a good deal, then he'll be happy *almost regardless of the pricing load you put elsewhere in the organization* because he has no idea what is a reasonable price for a cloud setup or API calls. But the CIO will know and recognize these prices and—if you've ensured they match up with her expectations—will probably pay them.

In that sense, you can look at your pricing like a conversation guide that the customer's buying committee can use to evaluate your proposal after you've left the room. Because the honest-to-God truth is that it's extremely difficult to truly evaluate the real value of any piece of enterprise software. Sure, it's probably not either a trillion dollars or zero, but arguments for and against can be made that keep that range quite wide.

So instead of evaluating the pricing and the purchase as a whole, which is really difficult if not downright impossible, the buying committee will evaluate the parts individually. The CIO will evaluate the cloud setup and API costs. The HR partner will evaluate the training costs. The head of compliance will evaluate the regulatory compliance setup. Each of them will likely realize that this particular line item will be loaded onto their budget. Even if it isn't, they will probably be responsible for judging whether or not the pricing of that item seems fair, which it is, of course, designed to be.

As each of these auxiliary stakeholders signs off their particular part of your pricing structure, they can now all look to the primary buyer, the head of widget production. If he likes his unit economics, whatever they are, he'll sign off too. From here on, you might have to do some negotiation posturing and contract work, but the sale is made.

The process of fitting your pricing structure to your customer's budget structure to maximize the "co-pay" from budgets that are ancillary to your primary target budget is what I call "Wallet structuring."

Is Wallet structuring a blank check that you can use to raise prices indiscriminately? No, but it is a powerful tool to help you work out *what kind* of complexity to add to your pricing architecture, as per the discussion of "whales" in the previous chapter. Especially if your solution started out in the mid-market SMB segment and is growing into an enterprise segment.

Some of the projects in which I, as a consultant, often unlock the most value come from software companies with around $100M in ARR who are finding it hard to keep growing. They are facing that problem because the ever-larger enterprise customers they are targeting are difficult to sell to, negotiate large discounts, and actually cost quite a bit to serve. Meanwhile, the SMB market where these SaaS businesses originally launched their product is now either too small to make a meaningful difference to them or clogged up with newly arrived competitors.

Often, the solution is to tap more budgets in their enterprise customers' budget structures. This generally creates a much better alignment with those customers, can reduce the blood sport of price negotiation, and can also increase ACV dramatically.

The process of finding line items to load on each of these ancillary budgets often amounts to asking the question: "What do we already deliver today for which there is an expectation to pay in our customer's organization?" If you deliver a solution of a meaningful size for $100K or more, there is a good chance that you can break down your delivery across features, services, reports, infrastructure, and so forth to come up with a list of fifty-plus items.

Group these into categories or themes, such as solution, IT infrastructure, services, reports, and so forth. Each of these should have a particular target budget in your customer's organization.

Now, you can sit down with your own team and go through each of these and inquire whether it would be reasonable to ask the customer to pay for this. You'll find that quite a few of the items (especially the ones where you have an obvious cost attached) might carry a high expectation to pay from your customer's side.

That's because many of these line items will resemble something for which the various stakeholders in the customer's organization are already paying—and that is precisely why there will be reference price points readily available in the market. This is especially true for all things IT infrastructure, where you can just look up online what all the large cloud computing providers are charging for storage and API calls, and so forth. It is also the case for a lot of services that require person-hours to deliver, such as support, premium account management, auditing, and so forth.

This is a crucial point: the expectation to pay for a certain item usually carries with it some sort of reference price point from your customer's side. Just as your polite plumber from the previous chapter can't charge you $140 for parking, when you know it's only $2/hour where you live, you can't charge your customers $10/#GB of storage because that would break your customers' perception that this is a pass-through cost for you. For many of these line items, there is a price level that you need to hit, one that resembles "what is usually paid for this."

However, it is very important to understand that this does *not* mean that you can't charge way above cost on those items. You just can't charge way above *perceived* costs. For example, cloud computing providers, such as Amazon Web Services, Microsoft Azure, and Google Cloud, have prices readily available online, but they will give their largest global customers very significant discounts. I worked with one global provider who got an 85 percent discount on list prices from one of those cloud providers, but we passed the list prices +5 percent on as a cost to customers, essentially marking up the cloud costs by +600 percent. Nevertheless, the customers still thought they were getting a really good deal.

Credit card fees and any other domain where a tech provider is openly basing their solution on or integrating with a third-party vendor are good candidates for such cost arbitrage. (No, not everyone is paying the same rates with Stripe or Braintree.)

Note that not all your customers will have the same perceived levels of costs. If you're running restaurant software, you can add $0.25 + 2.9 percent of every transaction when processing online credit card payments but only for smaller restaurants that assume everyone is paying these rates. Chain restaurants know the rates are negotiable and would try to estimate what you might be paying (I've seen rates as low as $0.05 + 0.2 percent for annual volumes over $1B).

Now, you have a list of line items for which you *could* charge. Whether you also *should* charge for them depends on how much complexity you need in your pricing architecture to properly discriminate between different customers and what those line items are.

So the process is as follows:

1. List the things you are currently delivering.

2. Group them into categories—each targeting a specific customer budget.

3. Evaluate each budget owner's expectation to pay for each line item in the category.

4. If a reference price exists in the market, note it. If it doesn't, estimate as well as you can.

Some of these line items will have flat fees, some transactional, and some will have metrics attached to them. Use common sense and put yourself in your customers' shoes when deciding.

The rule of thumb (which definitely has exceptions) is that the budget of your primary buyer should carry about 50–80 percent of the total price load. So if your ACV is about $500K a year, selling communication software to hospitals, load only the primary care budget with a relatively simple pricing model (e.g., a price per user, negotiated down). My estimate would be that you could add $100K–$500K of charges to the IT, HR, and other budgets in your customers' organizations. Or, at least, add these extra charges to new customers you get through the door.

MAKE THE CUSTOMER'S BUDGET PAY DIRECTLY FOR YOUR COSTS

One primary use of Wallet structuring is to ensure that your costs are covered and that your margins are maintained or even increased through all sorts of business scenarios.

I once helped a SaaS business that provided trading software to banks. They had about $50M worth of operational IT costs a year and a further $90M CapEx costs. Traditionally, they had simply charged their customers brokerage fees on the trading platform they provided, earning anywhere between $40K to $10M a year on each customer. But some customers used a far heavier and more complex solution than others, hammered the APIs harder, would open 100,000s of accounts just to close them again, and so forth. So my client estimated that about 20–35 percent of their customers were de facto loss-making when taking costs into account.

The problem was this: How do you ask customers to cover their own costs when it's not straightforward just what costs to attribute to them? After all, they were all running on the same platform.

The answer is this: cost proxies. We found, for example, that about 25 percent of the operational IT costs were in a bucket called "trading platforms." This covered everything from an on-site data center to cybersecurity software. I asked around inside the organization, "What drives this cost? What, if we got more of it, would make this cost go up?" The answer was "end clients," meaning that the more private retail customers the banks that were my client's customers had, the more my client would be spending on trading platforms. This is not trivial, as we could have got all sorts of answers back: number of trades, assets under management, third-party apps connected to the platform, etc.

Since we had about one million end clients, we simply divided the total trading platform cost of $12.5M (25 percent of the total $50M in operational IT expenses) by one million and got a "cost per end client" of $12.50 per year, which we rounded down to $1/month.

Now, the important thing to note here is that an end client isn't actually loading my client with another $12.50 of annual costs. That would imply causation. We don't really care, however, as long as we have a strong *correlation*. We simply need to find a metric that *tracks* the costs, not necessarily one that *causes* them.

We did similar exercises with other IT costs buckets, attaching costs to API calls, back-office operations, manual trades, and so forth until we had +90 percent of all IT costs covered.

Unlike the pure Wallet structuring exercise, where you simply list all the things you deliver, a cost-proxy exercise like this can come up with a metric (such as #EndClients) that isn't really something you deliver but nevertheless can be good for pricing insofar as it can communicate some value you bring or be openly used as a measure of the costs you have. (*"Well, we charge per end client simply because we know that's what is driving up our security and compliance costs. We actually don't make a margin on this. It's pure cost-covering."*)

There is almost always going to be a gap in this exercise where you don't track 100 percent of the cost, and you don't do it with 100 percent precision, but you can get close enough for it to be both operationally and strategically useful. Especially so if you forecast your costs at scale into the future and price to hit certain overall margins at set levels of ARR.

UNLOAD YOUR CUSTOMER'S CORE UNIT ECONOMICS

The final useful aspect of the Wallet-structuring exercise is that you can actually use it to make your product appear cheaper by shifting the pricing load away from your primary buyer's budget onto the other budgets in the customer's organization.

Take the trading software provider from earlier: by asking customers to pay for the software platform itself, we could, in some instances, offer better rates on brokerage, which mattered more to several clients. Even though they ended up paying the same net amount, the fact that it seemed cheaper on the core pricing measure that they cared about mattered quite a bit.

In a sense, you can consider a well-executed Wallet-structuring exercise to be like a premade internal budget negotiation on behalf of your customer. If you just load your entire SaaS license onto a single budget when negotiating with your customer, you are effectively asking the primary buyer to pay for 100 percent of a solution that might well have been carried across almost every budget in the organization, had they chosen to develop something internally themselves.

This subtly shifts the question from whether the customer's organization, as a whole, is willing to pay for your solution to a question of whether the particular budget you've decided to target can actually afford it. The pricing threshold is almost invariably lower if you end up asking the latter question. So don't.

COST-PLUS OR VALUE PRICING? BOTH!

If you've ever been in a discussion about whether to price according to the value you bring to the customer or simply do a markup of your costs in a "cost-plus" fashion, now you know the answer: do both.

Get the customer to pay for what they want, simply because they want it. That, in a sense, is gauging the pricing power of the demand for your product in and of itself. Then also get them to pay as large a proportion (or even *dis*proportion) of the cost to serve as you can.

Take a look at this (slightly edited) boardroom slide as a check-in halfway through the pricing structure design of a €100M ARR insurtech product:

CLAIMS MANAGEMENT SOLUTION

SOLUTION

Core Setup
- Core Solution Setup

Front Ends & Features
- Partner tools
- Scope: report, repair, book
- End-customer interfaces
- Communication lines

Add-Ons
- Integrations to repair network
- External data sources

IT INFRASTRUCTURE

Core Setup
- Security & continuity management

Usage
- Server usage & storage
- API calls
- Test servers & environments

Reporting
- ISAE 3000, critical outsourcing, etc.

SERVICES

Ticketed Services
- Support desk
- API incident desk

Time & Material Services
- Configuration services
- Bespoke development

Packaged Services
- Relationship manager
- Monitoring services

SALES PURPOSE	SALES PURPOSE	SALES PURPOSE
Discuss scope of solution	Communicate costs of delivery	Communicate costs of service

TARGET CUSTOMER BUDGET	TARGET CUSTOMER BUDGET	TARGET CUSTOMER BUDGET
Business OpEx – IT CapEx	IT OpEx – Compliance OpEx	Business OpEx – IT CapEx

PROFIT PRINCIPLE	PROFIT PRINCIPLE	PROFIT PRINCIPLE
Value pricing the solution	Cost scaling IT platform costs	Cost scaling service costs

DISCOUNTING	DISCOUNTING	DISCOUNTING
Possible	Not possible	Not possible

Figure 44: Splitting the overall solution into subcategories through packaging and pricing allows you to target specific subbudgets in the customers' wallet and provides targeted value propositions across value and fairness perceptions.

This product was relatively complicated and had high degrees of technical configurability and integration into the operations of the insurance company customers. On top of this came a host of services, from automated reporting to handheld account management. The SaaS provider had several people whose jobs were on-location with the customer to ensure the solutions ran properly.

Consequently, this pricing architecture had about 150 potential line items, and no two installations were the same. Bottom ACVs were around half a million euros.

Figure 44 shows how we designed each category of items, which we priced according to four core functions:

- **Sales purpose:** First, we decided how Sales should communicate around the category. The solution was where we knew we had demand, so that was where we communicated value. We showed nice interfaces, spent time on use cases, and calculated business cases for the customers, showing the money they'd make and save. Conversely, for IT infrastructure and services, we communicated the costs we'd have, driven by deep operational processes and so forth. This, of course, also has value, but we realized the customer has a satisficing mindset around these issues; unlike the solution, they don't drive demand.

- **Target customer budget:** Each of the three categories was assigned a target customer budget or budgets. We knew that the business line had to pay for the operational costs of not only the licenses of our SaaS platform but also many of the ongoing services. Because IT would carry operational IT costs, as well as bespoke development and configuration services, we could place the cost of integrating CapEx on IT, who would otherwise have a large CapEx expenditure developing it themselves. Finally, we knew we could ask Compliance to pay for much of the needed reporting.

- **Profit principle:** We used cost proxies to load costs onto IT infrastructure and services and decided to not mark these up but simply use the revenue generated here to break even— even if we priced the "solution" part at zero. In that way, we could then use the pricing of the "solution" category to determine the annual profits derived from the individual customer, since whatever we priced here would be pure profit as we'd already loaded all costs into the two other categories.

- **Discounting:** Finally, we guided Sales on how to negotiate pricing with customers to ensure that discounting supported the profit principles. Since IT and services were almost pure cost pass-through, it was easy to convince Sales to simply not give any discounts on these items. Conversely, Sales got more discounting power on the solution category, as well as a framework to calculate margins on the sale.

So we cost-plus price IT and services while we value-price the solution. That makes margins easier to work with and calculate on each individual sale, assuming cost proxies are properly attached to the pricing structure.

The fact that this pricing is part of Sales' communication strategy for your customers is actually a strength. By clearly communicating where in your pricing you are charging for value and when you are covering costs, you let your customers know what they are paying for and why.

This is easier to do in a complex product structure with apparent costs to the SaaS provider, but the principle holds true for simpler products and lower ACVs as well. The most commonly seen example is implementation costs, which almost always work on a cost-plus logic and, therefore, are only very rarely the object of price negotiation.

Next, Chapter 6 explains why price points are never absolute and explores how to set them relative to your competition and your customers' levels of sophistication.

SIX

PRICE POINTS

THE BEHAVIOURAL PRICING MATRIX

Prices are not high or low on an absolute basis—only in relation to something else. Or put differently: "Nobody has any real idea what anything should cost."

Let me give you an example.

Dan Ariely, a professor at Duke University specializing in behavioral economics, once handed out a blank piece of paper to each of the 200 students in his classroom. He then asked them to write the two last digits of their social security number in the top right-hand corner and handed out six items for inspection among the students: a textbook, a box of chocolates, a computer mouse, a keyboard, and two bottles of wine—one of which looked more expensive than the other.

He asked the students to write on their piece of paper what they would be willing to pay for each of these six items right now. He then collected the answers. Table 9 shows the average willingness to pay for the items, depending on whether the students' social security numbers ended in either the high end of 80–99 or the low end of 00–19:

Digits: 00–19	$8.64	$11.73	$8.64	$16.09	$12.82	$9.55
Difference	223%	220%	203%	246%	134%	116%
Digits: 80–99	$27.91	$37.55	$26.18	$55.64	$30.00	$20.64

Figure 45: Willingness to pay heavily affected by anchoring effect. Original price anchoring study done by Dan Ariely, Duke University. Here further developed with additional analysis on the base data set.

As you can see, the social security numbers apparently drive willingness to pay up by around 2x–3x. Perhaps graduate students are not as smart as they might imagine. But nevertheless, this should still raise some eyebrows. Especially when you consider the six items that were chosen aren't totally unfamiliar to most students; they regularly buy IT equipment, textbooks, and—presumably— wine and chocolate. They weren't asked to price a spare part for a vintage Porsche 911 or—even worse—a B2B SaaS solution. Still, the students with high digits at the end of their social security numbers were willing to pay a total of $197.92 for the six items compared to $67.47 for the group with low numbers.

Now, let's note a few interesting things from this experiment. First, even while there was a large discrepancy of several hundred percent in the difference between willingness to pay, nobody in either group stated they were willing to pay very high amounts for any of the items—like $10,000 for a bottle of wine (each group only had about fifty students in it, so a bid like that would have moved the average significantly).

Second, the two groups value the items very consistently relative to each other:

Digits: 00–19	$8.64	$11.73	$8.64	$16.09	$12.82	$9.55
Difference	223%	220%	203%	246%	134%	116%
Digits: 80–99	$27.91	$37.55	$26.18	$55.64	$30.00	$20.64
Market Share	14%	19%	13%	28%	15%	10%

Figure 46: While the overall willingness to pay is moved by 2–3x by the psychological anchoring, the relative prices within the market of goods are very stable. Source: Dan Ariely, Duke University.

Take the two bottles of wine. The "low" group values the cheaper-looking wine at $8.64 and the more expensive-looking bottle at $11.73—a 36 percent increase. The "high" group values the same bottles at $27.91 and $37.55, respectively, for a 35 percent increase. So the two groups only judge the bottles to be about 1 percent more relative to each other, even though the price levels for both bottles jump about 220 percent. If you consider each group of students a market, and the total amount that group is willing to pay for all the items combined as the market size, then you could say that the market share of each item is quite stable, even though the market size varies enormously.

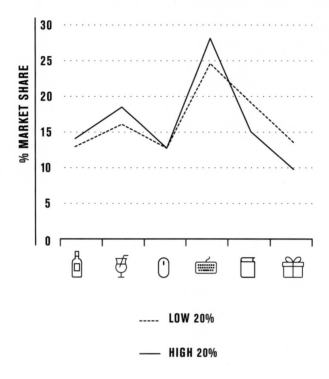

Figure 47: The individual share of each product of the total price for all products is very stable.
Source: Dan Ariely, Duke University.

The Dan Ariely study is a classic showcase of how the concept of "anchoring" works—the phenomenon that humans have a strong tendency to base any kind of estimate or judgment on the first piece of information we get, whether it is relevant or not (like random digits from a social security number) and then adjust that starting point with each new piece of information. This is one of the more robust and repeatable findings of behavioral economics, and it has many applications—such as the opening bid in a negotiation being far more determining for the outcome of the negotiation than the first counterbid.

Anchoring, however, is not a pricing strategy because you often don't get to determine what your customer is anchored to. They might be anchored to what they are paying now for the old solution you are bidding to replace. Or they might be anchored to the budget they set aside to solve this problem. Or to the market analysis that they've made of you and your competitors.

In the early days of my role as a pricing advisor, I spent a lot of time thinking about price anchoring and what determines customers' perceptions and evaluations of certain price levels. When can you "value price," and when do you have to take competitive pressure into account?

My conclusion was that prices are never "absolute." They are always "relative." And what they are relative to is driven by two primary factors: the presence of competition and the sophistication of your customer.

Sophistication, in this case, is an overall measure of how much information asymmetry exists between you and your customer. If your customer is very sophisticated, there is no asymmetry. But a customer with low sophistication knows less than you do, which creates different dynamics.

Customer sophistication is driven by four factors:

1. Frequency: How often they buy what you are selling.

2. Insight: How well they understand the value you can bring them.

3. Data: How much data they have access to on competitors' prices and products.

4. Priority: This is a bit of a fudge factor, but it reflects the fact that some customers simply care less about how much they pay.

To map these two forces (i.e., competitive pricing pressure and customer sophistication), I developed the Behavioural Pricing Matrix:

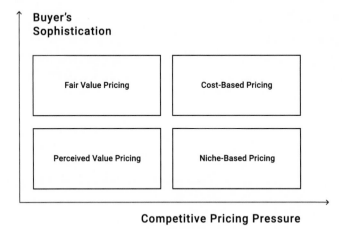

Figure 48: The Behavioral Pricing Matrix. A framework I've developed to understand what reference points a customer is likely to use to evaluate the price you present them with, depending on category commoditization and their sophistication.

The Behavioural Pricing Matrix maps out the four basic price-anchoring scenarios you get when you combine information asymmetry with competitive pressure: cost-based, niche-based, perceived value, and fair value pricing. Let's take a look at each of these in turn.

COST-BASED PRICING

I once helped a friend whose business was making cardboard boxes. He had four factories in China and specialized in producing boxes with two pieces, namely a bottom and a lid. His biggest customer was Procter & Gamble, where he dealt with a woman with the apt title "two-piece cardboard box procurement manager." I'm not kidding.

Imagine the depths of knowledge that a woman who had earned such a title would have about the whole world of two-piece cardboard box production. When you are dealing with a customer with that level of sophistication, you can scream "value pricing" until you turn blue in the face, but they will just walk out the door and buy the same goods from your competitor (if it's easy enough for them to find someone else who does what you do, which is certainly the case when it comes to making cardboard boxes).

In such a situation, with a sophisticated customer and plentiful competition, your customer's price anchor will be your cost base. They will not try to press your prices to zero. They know that is impossible. But they will try to press your profits to zero. If you are in that game, either get out or get more sophisticated than your customers. My take is that many payment solutions and digital signature providers are in this space.

Anchor: your costs.

NICHE-BASED PRICING

This is the situation where you have lots of competitors offering a relatively similar product, but your customers just aren't that sophisticated. Maybe they are not buying this sort of thing that frequently. Maybe access to good information on alternatives in the market is scarce and requires lengthy scoping and quoting processes. Or maybe they just really don't know in detail what they need or how the solution will affect their business.

If you are in a market like that, your customer will know that the price you are offering her probably isn't the best one available.

Because, despite being unsophisticated, she is aware that she is buying something for which there are many (too many!) vendors. What she'll try and gauge is whether the better price she might discover elsewhere in the market is justified by the added search cost she'll incur to find it. That is why hardcore price competition only works in transparent markets where customers are aware you are out there and can easily find you.

Niche-based pricing is often found in larger markets with lower ACVs, such as accounting software, design software, productivity software (e.g., Asana, Trello, Monday.com), and so forth. There is some differentiation among providers, but customers tend to not buy that often and stick with the solution they find for years. Your best option in this quadrant is to carve out a niche by positioning your product to reduce acquisition costs and decrease your prospective customers' sense that they can find a product that better fits their needs elsewhere (e.g., "We're the best wireframing solution for quick iOS mock-ups"). The more specific you are, the less likely it is that any further searching will get your target customer a better result.

Anchor: the transaction costs of finding a better price.

PERCEIVED VALUE PRICING

If you've ever spent just a couple of hours on Google reading about pricing, you'll have stumbled across the term "value pricing." The *Cambridge Dictionary* defines value pricing as "a way of deciding the price of a product, based on what customers think it is worth and on what they are willing to pay, rather than on what it costs to produce." According to the internet (and 99 percent of pricing consultants), you should apply that approach to pricing. Sure, if you are selling something unique to unsophisticated customers. In that case—and *only* in that case—your customers will try to relate the price you are asking to their perceptions of its value.

I think this was how AI was sold in the early 2010s, and how some blockchain technology is sold today (in 2022). Perceived value pricing is, however, not necessarily the best quadrant to be in, as customers' perceptions of value can be highly inaccurate and volatile. If you are truly trying to bring a brilliant, new, innovative technology to a blue ocean market, one of your main challenges will be explaining its value to your customers.

If they don't immediately "get it," you might be in deep trouble because they essentially *under*value your product. And I'm not a big fan of educating customers. To a degree, sure. When it comes to the finer details of your product as it compares to the alternatives, that's just part of selling. But you probably don't have the budget to truly lift your customers' overall level of sophistication. That takes the effort of a whole marketplace full of players. This is where a lot of "too early"-type companies fail. Their customers weren't prepared to pay.

Anchor: the customer's perception of your product's value—for better or worse.

FAIR VALUE PRICING

This, I think, is the right place to be for most enterprise software with higher ACVs. You sell something unique to an informed buyer. In that situation, your customer already knows all about the alternatives available, what they cost, what value they bring (or don't bring), and why they would prefer to buy from you. Because all those things are known, the customer will try to evaluate the price you quote them based on what is a fair exchange of value generated by the relationship, after having subtracted both your costs and theirs and factored in risk, opportunity cost, and so forth. Essentially, this is a gauge of fairness; they know they'd like to buy and don't have a whole lot of other options, but they would strongly prefer not to feel like you are taking advantage of the situation.

One of the lesser appreciated features of this quadrant is that it's the only one where it truly pays to educate your customer further. Give them honest comparisons between you and your competitors (showing that they truly can't get what they are searching for anywhere else), educate them further on the value of your product to their business (they know, but now they also know that you know), and so on.

Anchor: a fair share of the value generated by the relationship.

Now, not all of your product has to fit into one of these quadrants. It can span several. Maybe you offer a unique solution to large companies, so you have an "Enterprise" tier in the "fair value" quadrant. Here you should create pricing levels and price points based on business cases, analysis of unit economics, fair estimates of risk, implementation costs, and so forth, and then price in order to share the value fairly with your customers.

However, you might also have a Basic tier that you sell to SMBs, which has enough competition to be niche-based. Here your prices will be determined in relation to competing products, maybe charging a premium if you manage to capture a niche in the marketplace via positioning (e.g., "We are the preferred digital signature solution for small law firms").

Remember, the money is in the structure. If you've built the railroad, your monetization is going to be first dependent on your fencing of passenger vs. freight, to allow you to build different models for each. Next comes the packaging, which is then followed by the pricing architecture that maps on top of it. If you have gone that far, your structure is already doing all the heavy lifting to ensure you price the customer and not the product. "Second-class ticket, 500 miles" is going to be priced in a completely different dimension compared to "six tons of green bananas in a twenty-foot cooled container, 1,200 miles."

Add to that structure the "prices are relative" principle discussed earlier, and now we can start looking at the gritty details of actually setting price points.

There are basically four methods you can use to determine price points:

1. Internal expert judgment

2. Price experimentation and discovery

3. Customer surveys and interviews

4. Statistical prediction models

Let's take a look at each of these in detail.

INTERNAL EXPERT JUDGMENT

Internal expert judgment is simply asking your own team what they think customers would be willing to pay and then having a discussion about it.

Before you run this exercise, however, it helps to have a few things down: fencing, product packaging (i.e., "what jobs to be done" are we addressing), discount drivers, and Wallet structure.

(That is exactly why all these elements are covered before price points in this book.) With that information in hand, you can ask very succinct questions about pricing to your own team members.

I often use a Van Westendorp price sensitivity survey, which asks these four questions (in this order):

1. At what price would you consider the product to be so expensive that you would not consider buying it? (Too expensive)

2. At what price would you consider the product to be priced so low that you would feel the quality couldn't be very good? (Too cheap)

3. At what price would you consider the product starting to get expensive, so that it is not out of the question, but you would have to give some thought to buying it? (Expensive/ High Side)

4. At what price would you consider the product to be a bargain—a great buy for the money? (Cheap/Good Value)

It's easy for you to google how to handle the data inputs and interpret the results of a Van Westendorp—it's a classic pricing survey format, which has been around for thirty-plus years. Basically, the output looks like this:

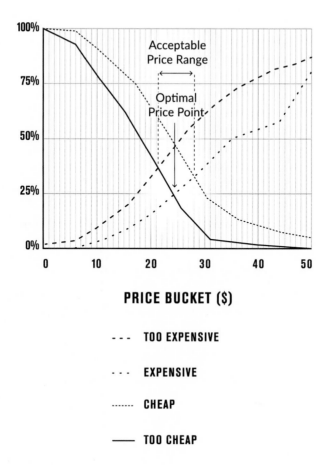

PRICE BUCKET ($)

- - -   TOO EXPENSIVE

· · ·   EXPENSIVE

·······   CHEAP

———   TOO CHEAP

Figure 49: Van Westendorf price sensitivity analysis. Study done by Uizard.ai and published on Medium.com.

The curves show "percentiles of respondents" for each of the four questions. So in the example output from Uizard, we can see that about 25 percent of respondents feel that a price of around $23.50 is "too cheap" (the green line), and another 25 percent feel it's "too expensive" (the blue line).

The core insight of the Van Westendorp price sensitivity meter is that it compares the overlap of "Uh, that feels expensive" with

"Hey, great bargain!" to find the *most acceptable* price points in your respondent group. That also makes it insensitive to large outlier-type answers. For example, if one respondent answers "$0" or "$1 billion," that's simply going to move the far ends of the percentile measures without affecting the sweet spot in the middle, which is what you are interested in.

Now, to make the Van Westendorp valuable for you, I suggest you run it across a matrix of your product packaging on one hand and your main discount driver on the other. For example, I ran an internal expert judgment Van Westendorp for Klara.com—a series B startup that provides patient communications solutions to doctors' practices. We had designed three tiers as part of their core packaging and knew that larger practices would be willing to pay a comparatively smaller dollar amount per healthcare practitioner (our primary pricing metric). We decided that a "small practice" would be five providers and a "large practice" would be fifty.

Here is a screenshot of the SurveyMonkey questionnaire we ran for the internal team:

3. TIERS:

CONSIDER A PRACTICE WITH FIVE PROVIDERS

Estimate the $-price per provider per month at which you think we'd see each of the below reactions for each of the three tiers.

A provider is any person seeing patients with an MD or DO as well as advanced practice providers or APPs (for example, a nurse practitioner, physicians assistant, or anaesthetist).

TIER 1

COMMUNICATE: Secure & smart messaging with your patients, staff, and peers.

TIER 2

AUTOMATE: Automate pre- & post-visit patient communication. EHR integration.

TIER 3

GROWTH: Improve scheduling & outreach workflows to increase patient appointments.

TOO EXPENSIVE
This tier would sell almost nothing at this price.

175 - per provider/month

175 - per provider/month

200 - per provider/month

SUSPICIOUSLY CHEAP
Our customers would second-guess the quality if it was this cheap.

30 - per provider/month

BARGAIN PRICE
The tier would be considered a "bargain" by most customers at this price.

10 - per provider/month
20 - per provider/month
30 - per provider/month
40 - per provider/month
50 - per provider/month
75 - per provider/month
100 - per provider/month
125 - per provider/month
150 - per provider/month
175 - per provider/month
200 - per provider/month
225 - per provider/month

THEY'D HAVE TO THINK ABOUT IT
At this price the practice might buy, but the price would be an issue and they'd have to think about it.

Figure 50: Example of a Van Westendorf price sensitivity survey targeted the internal product and sales department of a SaaS provider, split across the three available tiers in the packaging.

We asked the four Van Westendorp questions for each of the three core tiers in our packaging—and specifically for small practices of five providers. The next question in the survey was a repetition, only now for practices with fifty providers.

We surveyed across Sales, Customer Success, Management, and Product. The output looked like this:

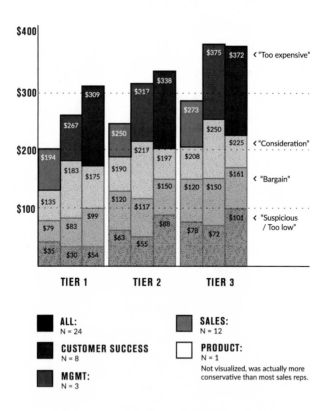

AVERAGE PRICE PER PROVIDER
FIVE PROVIDERS

Figure 51: Results of an internal Van Westendorf price sensitivity analysis for three product tiers broken down by department. As we can see, sales estimate a willingness to pay lower than customer success.

In the graphic, the respondents' answers are simply averaged for each team across the three product tiers and then stacked. As you can see, we have a general consensus that "Tier 3" is more expensive than "Tier 1," and Sales is more conservative with its pricing estimates compared to Customer Success and Management.

Now, let's look at the same responses for larger customers with fifty providers:

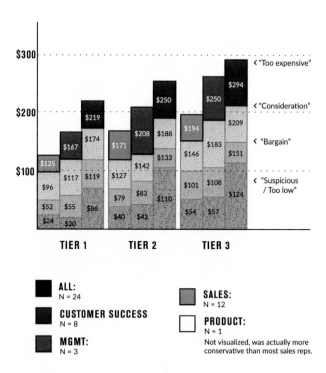

Figure 52: Same as above—but now specifically asked for largest customers with fifty providers. The difference allows us to gauge what discount should be given to larger vs. smaller customers.

This is about as much data as you can wring from a twenty-four-respondents survey, but if you have nothing else to go with, it provides you with a good starting point for what price points to at least test in the market.

Practically, I would usually recommend taking the "consideration" price point of the most conservative team (which is almost always Sales) as the list price and then allowing sales discounts down to the "bargain" price point of the most optimistic team (which is often Customer Success, followed by Product) and run a test phase with that. Doing that exercise with the Klara.com data produced the following figures:

PRICE POINTS INTERNAL SURVEY CONSIDERATIONS	TIER 1	TIER 2	TIER 3	#
Consideration price of most conservative team	$135	$135	$208	5 provider practices
Bargin price of most optimistic team	$99	$150	$161	5 provider practices
. . . .	. . . . .	. . . . .	. . . . .	. . . .
Consideration price of most conservative team	$96	$127	$146	50 provider practices
Bargin price of most optimistic team	$119	$133	$151	50 provider practices

Figure 53: The Van Westendorf results pushed into a spreadsheet. While we only have a total of twenty-four respondents to this survey, the structure of the survey allows us to gauge a clear range of reasonable prices between $96-$208 across product tiers, customer sizes, and internal department perspective.

As you can see, this works out well with the smaller customers, as there is a range of prices that are implicitly internally agreed upon as reasonable. For larger fifty-provider practices, however, the "bargain" price of the optimistic customer success department is higher than the "consideration" price of the pessimistic sales department. This happens all the time, especially for products and customer segments with which you don't yet have a lot of experience as an organization.

Think of the output here in a noise vs. signal context: each team member is trying to answer the pricing questions based on an on-the-spot synthesis of widely different information. Someone from Sales might base it on recent conversations with customers, experience from previous jobs, a chat with a colleague at a conference, and an email forward of some competitor's price list. Meanwhile, someone from Product might base their answers on a series of customer interviews, some business casework they did, a comparison to a competitor's product, and a survey they commissioned of churned customers.

The more internally consistent the answers from your various team members, the more you can assume that a real "signal" from the world is coming through, and you are actually getting useful information about what your customers would pay. But if the answers are all over the place, the "noise" is still far outweighing the useful information. You simply don't know yet.

So one of the main insights from a survey like this—even if you run it with only ten people in a startup—is to look for the level of consistency or *internal integrity* of the price points.

Yes, this can be heavily biased by the status quo (i.e., what you charge today) and, importantly, also by the asymmetry of the pricing information you get from your customers. As we saw in Chapter 1, they are likely to tell you only when they think the price is too high, not too low. That is why Sales are usually more price conservative than Customer Success and Product. There are other biases affecting internal price perception, but those two are the major ones. Assuming you are not one of the 1 percent of B2B SaaS companies that are actually overpriced, note that these two biases have the same directionality: both work to lower your internal perception of the customers' willingness to pay.

HOW TO USE THE RESULTS

Although they are useful and often provide real information, internal surveys are only a starting point. For that reason, you should use the output in combination with one of the other methods that I'll cover next to set price points. Or, if you only have internal surveys as an initial option, you should set your new price points up in a way that allows you to later use one of the other methods, the most immediate one being price discovery through testing and discounts.

For Klara.com, we combined all the methods; after completing the internal expert judgment process, we did large-scale market surveys and combined our findings with historical sales data to build a predictive model. Then we tested that model with field sales for three months to calibrate it.

That said, if we had had nothing to go on besides the internal surveys, I would probably have recommended price points like this:

PRICE POINTS BASED ON INTERNAL SURVEY	TIER 1	TIER 2	TIER 3	#
List price	$135	$190	$210	5 provider practices
Lowest price after sales discount	$100	$150	$160	5 provider practices
. . . .	. . . .	. . . . .	. . . .	. . . .
List price	$120	$135	$150	50 provider practices
Lowest price after sales discount	$95	$125	$140	50 provider practices

Figure 54: The differences in estimated prices across teams is turned into an experimental range through list prices and maximum discounts.

The five-provider prices are based on consistent estimates across the teams, so we have a higher degree of certainty here. That means that we want to: 1) aim high to counteract the downward pressure of default bias and asymmetric pricing information, and 2) give Sales some maneuverability in terms of discounts to test price points.

This is even more relevant for the fifty-provider prices, which brings us to our next price point method: price experimentation and discovery.

PRICE EXPERIMENTATION AND DISCOVERY

The second option you have for setting price points is experimentation and discovery: setting some price points, seeing what happens, and then adjusting accordingly.

That might sound like what your sales team is already doing now, but it's not. The reason *why* it's not is because Sales is not trying to discover better price points through setting up and running experiments in an attempt to sort signal from noise; they are just trying to close the customer in front of them.

You want to set up experiments that establish the following, in the following order:

1. Is the packaging right?
2. Is the pricing model right?
3. Are the price points right?

Generally, if you have a high ACV and a long sales cycle, you will have an easier time validating and getting feedback on number one and two in the list. Three is going to be quite hard. If you have a low ACV and a short sales cycle, the opposite is true: experimentation on price points is easy, but getting good feedback on your structure is far more difficult.

That is because your acquisition model determines the type of interactions you have with your customers. If you are selling $1M/year enterprise software solutions, your sales process is likely an outbound one driven by reps with deep industry experience who spend months or years talking to a customer before they close. If you are selling $10K/year document management software to the SMB segment, you likely have a sales team that processes mostly inbound leads. If you sell $50/month/user tooling through a self-service checkout on your website, you likely never talk to your customers.

The lower the ACV, the higher the number of customers, but the lower the level of engagement and dialogue you have with each customer. High ACV, meanwhile, means a high level of engagement with only a few customers.

ACV usually drives the acquisition model, so I normally base price experimentation on whether sales are driven by an outbound, inbound, or self-service process. Let's look at each of those in turn.

PRICE EXPERIMENTATION FOR OUTBOUND SALES

It's usually impossible to carry ACVs above $50K without outbound sales. To test price points in this setup, get your sales reps and product teams to heavily validate the structure of both your packaging and pricing model in tight collaboration with your customers; then test price points via sales discounts.

So if you think you can charge $50K a year for your top solution through a $25K flat fee plus $1K/user, send your sales team into the field and try to sell it for $40K flat and $1,500/user, but allow them to give up to a 50 percent discount. Run this for one sales cycle and then evaluate.

Let's say you closed the four deals you were supposed to over a quarter at $30K/$1,000#, $20K/$1,500#, $30K/$1,500#, and $25K/$800#. That would be excellent; only one sale was below your hypothesis price point of $25K/$1,000#. Next cycle, you might test $30K and $1,500/user, but with no discount on the flat and only a 33 percent discount available on the #Users.

Your goal would be to arrive at a price level where you would offer no permanent discounts that would affect ARR but only temporary discounts, free giveaways, or terms and conditions concessions (see the following chapter for more on discounts). That can be a stretch, as it relies on your packaging and pricing model being able to perfectly discriminate between customers on an individual level. So you might still need to have some degree of discounts available to close individual customers. Certain industries (e.g., enterprise edtech) can also have a tradition of large discounts.

For large ACVs above $50K, I'd say the maximum level of sales discounts should be 20 percent with a 10 percent median. Aim for zero percent—that would require both your packaging and your pricing model to be well aligned with your customers.

Since you've already done your homework by breaking down your offering into functional, service-related, and commercial features and reassembling them around jobs to be done, you should theoretically already be confident that there is a good product-market fit for your packaging. I say "theoretically" because, in reality, there is almost never time to pre-validate every last detail of an offering with customers before it hits the market. So you need to have a tight relationship between Product, who were likely the team in charge of the pre-validation of the product before the market test, and Sales, who were responsible for the first real market test.

Here is what usually goes wrong: Sales wants to solve any problem with discounts, even if the problem with the offering is not with the suggested price points but rather with one of the structural levels (i.e., the packaging or pricing model). That can be a really expensive issue, especially as some structural problems might simply lead to some customers not buying, regardless of discounts.

I once worked with a large OEM that was selling $25K machines to large contract cleaners and facility managers. Its typical customer would spend $2K–$300K on machines every year in a region but would lose track of where they were during normal operations and would thus have to purchase new ones simply because those they bought last year went missing. This was in 2018, before cheap IoT connectivity devices, so the OEM needed a low-cost solution to get their customers onto their IoT platform, which didn't require a $30/month GSM box.

Their idea was simple and beautiful: send QR-code stickers for free and develop a mobile app that allows the machines to be scanned and tagged. Then, the on-site operator could input identifying information, such as the serial number, and headquarters would now know where the machine was.

Simple and effective. However, the OEM was worried that "someone in Mozambique" (that was the actual phrase used) was simply going to order a million of these QR stickers for no reason. So they decided to charge $0.05 per QR-code sticker, just to cover the cost.

A few weeks prior to the pilot launch of their new software, I happened to talk to a regional manager of ISS, the largest cleaning company in the world and the biggest customer of the OEM I was helping. I asked him what he thought about the $0.05 stickers, and he promptly replied, "That's totally fair, of course. Five cents is probably just the cost price, but then we just can't buy it." It turned out that ISS's company policy was that the total cost of ownership had to be calculated and managed on a machine level, which meant that any cost had to also be booked and accounted for on a machine level.

So if they ordered 20,000 QR-code stickers, they would get an invoice for $1,000, which some poor soul in accounting would then have to manually split into 20,000 distinct bookings and place in

20,000 separate sub-accounts in their bookkeeping system. The whole process would take months.

For live sales tests with larger ACV deals, the rep who is trying to close the sale should pay special attention to what I call "the quality of the no." Of course, in any sales test period, you will pay attention to how many sales you can close compared to the total number of prospects. But taking account of the quality of the no means that you should probably pay even more attention to the customers who don't buy and ask them why they didn't.

If they use phrases like "The product seems nice, but the timing isn't right" or "I don't know if it's for us" or "I like that feature, but..." or "I don't understand why you've..." or any other language that is clearly associated with some form of lack of immediate demand, then you have some sort of structural problem with either your packaging or your pricing model. If, however, they use language like "The product is really great; we just don't have $45K in the budget for this, even though we really need it," then it's likely just a price-point issue.

It's crucial to understand that the key to running price experiments at high ACVs is being able to distinguish between two types of "no." The first is a rejection of the structure, which essentially shows itself as a lack of demand. The second is a refusal to settle at a particular price point, despite the presence of demand. See Chapter 7 for more on "the quality of the no."

If you get pushback on price in a sales test, negotiate like hell to close at as high a price point as possible—but be willing to use the whole range of discounts you've allowed yourself in this sales test. Or, if you are like any other startup out there, settle at any price that grows ARR and will get you closer to the next funding round.

That also means you should probably test out rather high-price points (i.e., ones that you internally think are quite high but that conversely have significant discount potential). If you think $50K is right, test the $40K–$75K range. If you really don't have a clue, then test a very wide range.

In the Klara.com case, for example, we tested price points for add-ons like "Advanced Surveys" and "Payments" with price points five times higher than what had previously been charged. We also allowed regular sales reps to give up to a 50 percent discount, sales managers 75 percent, and the chief sales officer 90 percent.

PRICE EXPERIMENTATION FOR INBOUND SALES

When it comes to companies that are mainly dependent on inbound sales, I suggest testing at two levels: the pricing page of your website and the inbound sales conversation. Start with a lowish price point, and then spend an entire sales cycle optimizing the pricing page for lead conversion. Be laser-focused on matching the communication of jobs to be done in your packages to the conversations your sales reps have with your customers. For example, offer discounts in the 0–30 percent range—lower than those you would offer for pure outbound sales.

Why? Well, there are three main differences in price-point testing between inbound and outbound sales. First, inbound leads are already prequalified by your marketing, so assuming you have some form of public packaging and pricing the customer has already checked out, there should be a lower likelihood of being misaligned with the customer on structural issues related to packaging and the pricing model.

Second, it's way harder to tell if the customer is rejecting the structure of your packaging/pricing or the price point itself in inbound sales. You usually are not face-to-face with the customer; you will have fewer conversations; the conversations you do have will be more scripted; and the product is less configurable at mid-low ACVs, so there is less exploration of the use case by the sales rep.

Finally, the ACV on inbound sales is likely to be significantly lower than on outbound, so the risk of losing any particular customer is probably bearable.

So you lower the discount range because prequalification entails less discounting being necessary, and the lower level of customer interaction can mean that the sales rep misinterprets a structural no as a price no, which leads them to offer discounts when they shouldn't. And you can afford to lose the sale (yes, you really can).

In this first cycle, where you are focused on optimizing for lead generation from your pricing page, your conversion rate on inbound leads should be high. Remember, prospects have already been qualified by marketing and have seen your pricing on your website before they get in touch. So if they get in touch, they are ready to buy.

If you are really happy with your results from this first cycle, and you can see you are hitting all your revenue and growth targets, just keep your prices and start working on reducing discounts. If you are curious about what the market is actually willing to pay, raise the prices on your website by about 20 percent and test for another sales cycle.

Here is an example of how that might turn out:

INBOUND CONVERSION	MARKETING SPEND	LEADS TO WEBSITE	INBOUND LEADS	NEW CUSTOMERS	LIST PRICE	AVG. % DISCOUNT	AVG. ACV	NEW ARR GAIN
1ST CYCLE	15,000 USD	1,000	50	20	5,000 USD	20%	4,000 USD	80,000 USD
2ND CYCLE	15,000 USD	1,000	40	18	6,000 USD	25%	4,500 USD	81,000 USD

Figure 55: Example breakdown of price testing list prices across sales cycles. While the net ARR outcomes are very close, there is real and measurable difference at all steps in the funnel leading up to this.

When reviewing the previous example, bear in mind that you are trying to optimize for net ARR gain as compared to your top-of-funnel marketing spend. That's why we squeeze another 1.25 percent ARR gain out of a 20 percent list price increase from $5K to $6K. The extra list price is simply eaten up by a combination of a lowered lead velocity from the website to inbound leads, as well as a higher average discount. Conversion rate drops from 2.0 percent to 1.8 percent in the overall funnel, with a 20 percent drop in Step 1 but an increase by 12 percent in Step 2—it is a common pattern to shift conversion back into later stages of the funnel as prices increase.

WHY 1.25 PERCENT IS MASSIVE

Even though a net ARR gain of 1.25 percent may seem very small, it would actually be a great result. First of all, 1.25 percent is 1.25 percent. If you run this logic over the course of four, eighteen-month funding rounds as a startup, it means you'll get a +5 percent increase in total ARR at the time of exit as the simple, nominally higher ARR in each funding round compounds, enabling you to raise more money to push into CAC in the next round.

Now, add in the much-improved unit economics on a customer level. In the second cycle, we increase ACV +12.5 percent, which is probably going to increase your CLV similarly because churn is actually unlikely to increase, since you're now selling to the much smaller base of 40 inbound leads who've already prequalified themselves to the higher pricing on your pricing page.

CAC should actually go down because you are now processing only 40 inbound leads and not 50 for the same net ARR growth. This might not kick in immediately in your first test cycle, but it will if you choose your growth trajectory at this higher ACV. If we simply assume that you spend a similar amount on inbound sales efforts as you do on marketing, it is a huge deal to close the same net ARR with only 80 percent of the effort (from 50 to 40 leads processed). Eighty percent effort on half your CAC is a 10 percent decrease in overall CAC.

So with a +12.5 percent increase in CLV and a –10 percent cost in CAC, your CLV/CAC is actually boosted by 25 percent (i.e., from 4.0 to 5.0). That is massive.

It's not only massive because you now have a better business but also because your funding partners will notice. A +25 percent increase in CLV/CAC is likely to mean at least +10 percent in the multiple that is being applied at your funding rounds—taking a 10x multiple to 11x or a 20x multiple to 22x. A similar effect is likely in a stock market or private equity context, but of course, capital markets are all fickle.

Whatever your sources of growth capital, if you raise +10 percent capital in each round, that should mean you can grow at a +10 percent rate compared to whatever rate you were previously growing at. (I know money doesn't solve everything, but you can also trade capital to increase runway and allow for more mistakes, etc.) Even setting aside the fact that the increased growth itself will further boost the multiple in the second funding round and beyond, this +10 percent alone compounds across your four funding rounds for a whopping +46 percent. Now multiply on the base +5 percent net ARR gain on 1,000 leads, and you have a +54 percent ARR over the course of six years and four funding rounds.

That's the difference between a $650M company and a unicorn. And it can be achieved by using pricing to tweak unit economics—the net ARR gain is a side effect.

You can now choose to test yet another price point increase in a third cycle (e.g., from $6K to $7K in list prices), or you can start working on raising the executed ACV by reducing the discounting available to your sales reps. This really comes down to the feedback you are getting from Sales. If you think your product-market fit is great but your price really just is at too high a level, it's time to stop and work on discounts. In any other case, test the next level of price points.

Let's assume you run two more cycles that look like this:

INBOUND CONVERSION	MARKETING SPEND	LEADS TO WEBSITE	INBOUND LEADS	NEW CUSTOMERS	LIST PRICE	AVG. % DISCOUNT	AVG. ACV	NEW ARR GAIN
1ST CYCLE	15,000 USD	1,000	50	20	5,000 USD	20%	4,000 USD	80,000 USD
2ND CYCLE	15,000 USD	1,000	40	18	6,000 USD	25%	4,500 USD	81,000 USD
3RD CYCLE	15,000 USD	1,000	38	17	7,500 USD	27%	5,475 USD	93,200 USD
4TH CYCLE	15,000 USD	1,000	36	15	9,000 USD	28%	6,480 USD	97,200 USD

Figure 56: Above example now extended with two more sales cycles.

That would be a great result, of course. It also is far from uncommon. In my experience, most B2B SaaS products have significant unlocked pricing power if their packaging and pricing models are well designed. If net ARR gain drops from one test cycle to the other, make a judgment call. A higher ACV is preferable (check the sidebar if you want to know why), but of course ARR growth is king. If you believe your sales reps honestly could do better on discounts, or if your cost structure is significant so a price increase also means a significant profit margin increase, that could make the case for going with the higher ACV despite the lower net ARR gain. Then work toward bringing conversion rates up and discounts down at these price points in subsequent cycles.

The core process is relatively simple: experiment across sales cycles and measure the entire funnel. Use discounts in the 0–30 percent range to allow sales to discover real willingness to pay. Match CAC to net ARR gain. And stop or pull back when it's obvious that you should.

PRICE EXPERIMENTATION FOR SELF-SERVICE SALES

Price experimentation for self-service sales works just like inbound sales, except without the discounts and the opportunity to talk to customers.

Start by working on your marketing conversion up to the point where customers are presented with a price. Then measure for a full sales cycle before you test a new price point. If net ARR gain is accretive, test another price increase. Repeat.

Use your judgment to establish what price points to test. Establish which quadrant of the Behavioural Pricing Matrix your product is in and work from there. For example, if you are in the upper left, base your price on a business case analysis of your customers. If you are in the lower right, focus on competitor prices, adjusted for the strength of your brand and niche.

If your analysis says your price should be +500 percent, test that; the risk-reward is heavily asymmetrical in your favor. However, unless you've been tracking price sensitivity for years and have very good data to say otherwise, never test anything below a +20 percent increase.

There are two main reasons for that. First, you are likely underpriced, and you need to address that faster with big steps. Second, your volume of sales and leads is unlikely to be big enough to give you clear statistical insights into customers' price preferences if you move ahead in small steps. Despite anxiety concerning pushback from the market, realize that what you want is a "big reaction," so that you will know the result of your test. Maybe conversion will stay unaffected or maybe it will take a big hit. Either way, you'll get a clear signal from your customers whether your price is "still OK" or not.

Now, what you also need to do is set up some form of information gathering exercise that listens to the grapevine of customer chatter. If you have a community of users or similar, they are going to be upset that you are changing prices. Ignore that—or simply be transparent about what you are doing—but don't take pushback here as information. It's noise, as those users are anchored on past prices and focus much more on the rate of change than on the absolute price points, which is what you are testing for.

Instead, find and talk to genuine new prospects and customers. Try to tease out whether there are issues with the overall structure of the product packaging and the pricing model or the price points themselves. Realize that this qualitative part of your price testing gives you much more true information compared to just making slight changes in your prices, unless you onboard 500+ paying customers for each test.

This, in my experience, is what makes price-point testing in self-service actually the hardest. It is so easy to just try and turn it into a numbers game that you blind yourself to the fact that price points are downstream from your price structure. You're much better off investigating and working on the structure before you tweak the price points.

CUSTOMER SURVEYS AND INTERVIEWS

Customer surveys are great if you know how to use them—and how not to. The main issue is that it's much harder to get quality respondents than you'd think.

If you have 300 customers you want to survey and really lean into the process with support from account managers and Customer Success to chase responses on a survey, you are lucky if you get 50—or about a 15 percent response rate. If you have 3,000 customers and don't chase them, you are lucky if you get 50 responses. Anything above 1 percent is pretty good.

For that reason, I actually don't think surveys are a good source of quantitative information. You are not getting enough respondents to do anything remotely statistically significant, and the sampling bias implicit in the low response rates is potentially so large that it casts serious doubt on the results, even if you managed to get over 1,000 responses to a survey.

Instead, treat surveys as a format of structured, qualitative input, part of which might be asking respondents to provide you with answers in the form of numbers.

Bearing that in mind, here are the segments I usually use in customer surveys:

1. A MaxDiff ranking of twelve to fifteen select functional and service features, a few of which are roadmap features

2. A simple ranking of two to five commercial features

3. A simple ranking of potential pricing metrics

4. A Van Westendorp price sensitivity survey

5. Lots of free text fields and open-ended questions

Position your questions as a product survey. Tell your customers you are trying to build the best possible solution for them, and you need help to figure out what features to develop and why. Include roadmap features—or the main features of your competitors' offerings—to gauge how they stack up against your current feature set.

Split out commercial features in a separate section and follow with open-ended "why?" text-box questions. For example, "Why did you rank 'predictable pricing' as the most important feature?" Use the same format for asking about pricing metrics. Here, I usually formulate as follows: "Today, we price per square foot, but some customers have asked us for other formats. So assuming the price is fair, please rank from 1—most preferred to 4—least preferred the following four ways we could price as you see them." The "fair" part is inserted to signal to the customer that you are looking for their guidance on *structure*—not price levels.

That is the key with pricing surveys: when you get to the "how much" part, your respondent is quite likely to try and game the survey and not answer truthfully. The Van Westendorp format tries to accommodate this by the sequence of the four questions, starting with asking what the respondent would *not* pay. Further, since you are probably asking either existing customers or respondents who have some form of relationship with your product, you have a huge sampling bias here. They are going to be preconditioned to give an answer that is very close to your current price points. The output, therefore, can only be used directionally—up or down. Don't try to squeeze some statistical "optimal" price point out of a survey.

This direction of the Van Westendorp, together with the output of preferences on the MaxDiff in the feature part of your survey, should give you a good indication of whether prices can go up. So if the new roadmap features are ranking well against existing features—and the Van Westendorp survey didn't rule out price increases—use that to set new price levels and engage in price discovery through sales testing, as explained in the previous section.

I know it's counterintuitive to use surveys primarily as a qualitative tool and not a quantitative one, especially as everyone wants to be "data-driven." Just don't confuse that with "quant-driven." Yes, at the end of the day, a price is a number. So intuitively we should be able to calculate something, right? Yes, but remember: garbage in, garbage out. Until you have the foundation to do real optimization, don't be tempted.

STATISTICAL PREDICTION MODELS

When I talk about statistical price modeling, I refer to the kind of predictions that tell you who will buy what at what price.

At its most basic level, a simple survey analysis, such as a Van Westendorp price sensitivity meter, tells you that "at ten dollars per user, 85 percent of respondents don't seem to rule out buying." But which 85 percent? And will they buy? And what about at $9.99? Or what if you introduce a new product or repackage the existing offerings?

You can attempt to model price elasticities in Excel, but it can cover only a very small subset of your potential offerings and prices, doesn't take cross elasticities of demand into account (where the price of one product affects the willingness to pay for another), and only handles a point-in-time analysis as it's almost impossible to set it up to update easily as new data comes in.

This is where you need to spin up a dedicated piece of price-modeling software. This is a rapidly evolving field, but here are the conceptual basics that you need to understand the potential and evaluate if this is for you.

At its core, a statistical-pricing model should be able to tell you with reasonable precision the likelihood that a given customer will buy a given product at a given price. It's a prediction game.

So for example, if you have 100 leads of varying sizes coming through your funnel and being presented to your three product tiers (which are priced at $10, $20, and $30/user respectively), a statistical price optimization model should be able to tell you with a <5 percent margin of error the likelihood that a customer buys and which of the three tiers that customer will buy for each of the 100 customers. This is shown in the following table.[10]

INBOUND CONVERSION	LEADS	$ PER #USER	TOTAL #USERS	TOTAL MRR
Total Leads	1,000	30 USD	10,000	300,000 USD
Sales of Tier 1	45	10 USD	225	2,250 USD
Sales of Tier 2	35	20 USD	350	7,000 USD
Sales of Tier 3	20	30 USD	400	12,000 USD
Lost Sales	900	-USD	9,025	- USD
TOTAL SALES				21,250 USD

Figure 57: Because most SaaS products are priced using some pricing metric, any analysis of price elasticity that predicts conversion rate has to take into account how many units—e.g., #users—each converted customer is buying.

There are two major ways in which statistical modeling differs from basic Excel-based models. The first is the way it treats customers. The second is the way it works from an operational standpoint.

10   A 5 percent margin of error means that if it predicts a 20 percent conversion rate overall, the actual conversion rate should fall within the range of 19-21 percent for products for which you already have sales data. If you can accept a wider margin of error, don't bother with prediction models at all. Simply run trial-and-error testing and surveys. If you do commit and do the work to set up price-modeling software, work toward a sub-2 percent margin of error, which is achievable even with under 500 customers.

Let's take a look at those differences in more detail below.

A CUSTOMER SHOULD BE A SEGMENT OF ONE

Statistical modeling differs from basic Excel-based exercises on a computational basis by treating each customer as just that: one customer, with all their individual qualities, preferences, history, etc. This is a massive breakaway from the traditional marketing-prediction methodology, which works with "segments" and "personas" to make sense of large and unwieldy data sets and problems.

In statistical modeling, each customer is considered to be a composition of underlying attributes (such as size, type, geography, and customer status), which produces data rows (such as "Miami-based law firm with twenty #Users, currently on the Freemium Plan"). Each customer attribute and attribute set (i.e., the combination "Miami" and "law firm") is then given a particular preference score for each of your available features and feature sets. So "law firm" might have a high preference score for your software feature "live data customer credit risk," but a low preference score for your service feature "legal hotline."

Modeling preferences for sets of attributes and features is important, as some features can have more value together than they do individually (e.g., the features "single sign-on" and "ERP integration"). Similarly, customer attribute sets can have preference impacts beyond those of individual attributes, which need to be modeled (e.g., "US" and "law firm" could have a high preference score for "live data customer credit risk," while "France" and "law firm" might have a low preference score, as French lawyers have a tradition of working on upfront retainers, making the credit risk a nonissue for them). Importantly, that low preference score is not correlated to either "France" or "law firm" but to the set of the two together.

These preferences can be generated through analysis of your sales and CRM data (known in pricing parlance as "revealed preferences") or survey data (known as "stated preferences"). Good price-modeling software should integrate the two to create a strong, unified model of customer preferences across all available data sources. Price is simply considered a feature in this mix so that each customer attribute and attribute set has a preference for each set of price-feature combinations, presumably with a lower preference for higher-price points.

So for any potential customer who fits within your described parameters of customer attributes, you should be able to determine their preference for any bundle of features at any price and in relation to any other bundle of features at any other price. The percent probability of whether a given customer would buy is triangulated based on the actual conversion rates you have from your current sales data, where actual live customers either bought or didn't buy a live offering at a live price.

Oversimplified, if today you are selling Bundle A at $10 to Customer X at a 20 percent conversion rate, but your model shows that Customer X will have a 20 percent higher preference for Bundle B, the model might predict a 24 percent conversion rate for Bundle B at $10 and a 20 percent conversion rate at $12.

That means the prediction of whether each customer will buy (and what they will buy) should be based on that individual customer's composition of attributes and how those attributes have choice tendencies (i.e., preferences) toward features—not on segments or personas. Further, this allows you to model the impact on prices based on a distribution that takes into account the fact that not all customers are created equal. So instead of working with 1,000 customers, with an average of ten users each, you work with 1,000 customers with different #User counts, based upon the actual underlying distribution of users in the market you are trying to model. This data should be extractable from your CRM data.

In the example table, Tier 1 customers have an average of five #Users while Tier 3 customers have an average of 20 #Users each. This makes a Tier 3 customer 12x as valuable (4x users, 3x price), which is absolutely critical when you are trying to revenue or profit optimize.

SAMPLE SIZE AND METHODS

A common concern I encounter when working with SaaS companies is that the sample size of existing customers or survey respondents is much too small to power a significant statistical analysis. With just five binary customer attributes, ten features, and five price points, there are more than 1.1 billion potential permutations. This makes simple regression analysis and subsequent statistical significance of correlation a nonstarter if you want to consider all possible scenarios.

The classical solution was simply to not consider all possible scenarios but instead focus on a small handful (i.e., less than ten), which makes the task of gathering data for a regression analysis of price elasticities much more feasible. These elasticities were then built into Excel calculators that extrapolated narrow-band elasticities based upon the ten investigated scenarios onto more scenarios, with the caveat that "the statistical significance of results outside price range $X to $Y is severely diminished." (In other words, garbage in, garbage out.) If you wanted to predict prices outside the original ten scenarios, you had to gather data for those scenarios, rerun your model, etc.

That approach is now old hat.

Instead, today's most advanced statistical-price modeling looks at the prediction of conversion rates as an information problem and tries to solve it with Bayesian-inference modeling. Basically, this approach starts with a baseline assumption (e.g., a 50 percent chance of a sale, if nothing else is known, or your existing conversion rate) and then updates the probability of a sale based on each new piece of information. If no information is available, the baseline is assumed. Additional algorithms and assumptions are usually added to "round off" the predictions and handle various special cases, such as behavioral biases.

When running modeling tests on ultra-large datasets (e.g., ten billion data points) and then rerunning the predictions using only small random samples of that dataset, about 95 percent of the precision of the large data set can be reached with only one hundred random data points.

So yes, more data is better. But if you approach the problem correctly, there are vastly diminishing returns on sample size after the first few hundred customers or survey respondents.

GENERATING OPTIMUMS

Price optimization happens when you run several predictions, compare them for outcomes, and implement the one you believe will best fulfill your objectives.

Will Bundle A generate more MRR at $10/user or $11/user? What if we introduced Bundle B at $15? If you can predict each, you can rank them. That means if you can predict 100 or 100 million, you can rank all of them based on which one generates the highest MRR or highest profit from a given set of prospective customers.

Usually, it makes sense to work with certain thresholds when generating optimums as pricing normally needs to balance several objectives. This could, for example, include picking the best price-product combination, from an MRR growth perspective, that still maintains a given profit margin. Or you might feel that you have a commitment to a community of users who requires you to keep your freemium product, even though the price modeling tells you it would generate more MRR growth to remove it from your packaging. Or you could have a market-share strategy that dictates that you grow the number of users or customers now, only to monetize them later as your product matures.

While all these constraints and considerations are absolutely fair game, the discussion of them also ought to change as you introduce price modeling. Because now you can begin to estimate their true cost.

Take the freemium example, a hot topic in almost any SaaS business, whether it is a startup or an established company. Proponents will usually believe wholeheartedly in the freemium model's critical necessity in terms of bringing new leads to the paid product at a very low CAC. Skeptics will agree but argue that the freemium product cannibalizes the paid product to an extent that does not justify the lowered CAC it helps generate. You can run this argument a million times with no clear resolution until you actually commit to a quantified prediction of sales in each scenario.

When you do that, you will find there is also a clear dollar difference between the two scenarios. If, say, the packaging with a freemium product generates $10K less MRR out of every 1,000 prospects compared to the non-freemium packaging, then I'd argue you ought to add those $10,000 to the CAC of the customers who do convert in the freemium scenario and then do the CLV/CAC comparison. The same kind of analysis can be run with every constraint or adjacent objective you might have, where their opportunity cost can be quantified when compared to the highest-performing MRR or revenue-growth scenario under no constraints.

If you want to really geek out on this, you can, of course, create functional relationships between these objectives, visualizing profits as a function of revenue, percentage of market share as a function of revenue, etc.

OPERATIONAL OPTIMIZATION

There are two bottlenecks to generating value from price modeling: the rate and quality of the data you put into the model and the operational implementation of the results and insights you get out of the model.

Here is my recommendation: get the data input to an absolute minimum usable standard, then focus on getting really, really good at the operational implementation. I repeat, do not proofread the stone tablets. Just get them off the mountain.

The reason is that data quality and volume drive two things and two things only: precision on individual predictions and the number of different predictions you can make (e.g., with more data you can break down the predictions by sales channel, market, customer types, etc.). ★ ❏ ❱ ❄ ❖ ❄ ❏ ❦more predictions require more implementation, and if precision meets your baseline criteria of <5 percent variance, then—by definition—everything below that will have faster and faster diminishing returns. Even the most sophisticated optimization of price and product has zero impact unless it's actually the offering being sold to customers; implementation is always the bottleneck.

There is a deeper point to be made here, which is that the true value of price optimization doesn't lie in the initial optimum being generated but rather in your newfound ability to generate optimums when you need them. Because in six months your product will have changed, your competitors' products will have changed, relative market share and brand recognition will have changed, you will have started to sell to new types of customers, and so on. In other words, every variable in your model will have altered: customer attributes, features, and the preference relationships between them. So you need to update the model with new data, recalibrate, and recalculate.

With good price-modeling software, the data should flow directly from your CRM and accounting systems into your model, and Product should either be making their feature preference surveys directly via the price-modeling software or have an easy integration to feed survey data into the model. But if implementing a change in packaging and pricing is a three-month-plus project for you that has a significant cost in terms of development, marketing, and internal process change, then you are unlikely to make that change again after six months—even if the model says there is another 20 percent annual growth to squeeze out of your product.

Moreover, the prediction model doesn't really start to get good until you've actually pushed the change into the market and fed new sales and CRM data back into the model. This iterative cycle of prediction—implementation—measurement—calibration—prediction is critical for generating value from your pricing over time.

The cycle length measured in days is what you should focus on. Even for very large ACVs above $50K, you should be able to run a cycle in six months, assuming you get one hundred-plus customers a year. For anything below $50K ACV, you should be able to shorten the pricing iteration cycle to three months. For $10K and below, you should be able to run monthly cycles.

So if you have 100 units of execution power, spend 10 of them on the initial model and 90 on pushing the results out to your sales channels as quickly and smoothly as possible. Once you hit the iteration cycle lengths, you can redistribute and spend more energy on data sources and generating new analyses.

Even better, get really good at executing price changes before you start statistical-predictive modeling. Simply use redesigns, surveys, and testing, and then add your predictive model to feed this implementation engine.

Now that you've worked out your price points, the next priority is to validate them. Chapter 7 shows how you can do that by working with your current and potential customers to achieve good pricing that is in everyone's best interests.

SEVEN

VALIDATION

CUSTOMERS WANT YOU TO HAVE GOOD PRICING

After you've worked out your product and pricing models, structured your wallet, and set your price points, you'll want to check that you've got all that right. There are generally four ways to build your confidence that you've got good pricing:

1. It makes sense to you.

2. Customers have told you it makes sense in interviews.

3. You have good survey data to indicate that it makes sense.

4. You have actually sold products at those prices in the market.

But before diving into each method, it pays off to realize a core truth: customers want you to have good pricing. This doesn't mean they want you to be expensive, but rather that they want a good method of exchanging value with you.

I actually think the term "product-market fit" is misleading because real traction only comes when you have a really good overall commercial model, which covers your acquisition model, your product model, your pricing model, and your service model. While your product is the source of demand for your customers, each of the other three sub-models in your overall commercial model has the potential to create endless amounts of friction and, ultimately, derail your train.

And that is something your customers most certainly do not want.

Customers want to buy a product that solves a clear job for them, using a sales channel that balances their particular needs for speed, convenience, and trust, while paying in a way that is fair and transparent. More importantly, you also want all those things, so your interests are clearly aligned with those of your customers. This means on the structural level at least, you can have an open and honest conversation with your customers about your pricing and any other part of your commercial model.

Think of the reverse: you have a really good product, sold by a prime sales team, but with a poor pricing model that really doesn't match the value of individual purchases, creates undue risk for your customer, and so forth. Your customer would want you to fix this, to allow them to buy, because the whole point of buying something is that you want "it" more than the money you are parting with. The customer is better off after the purchase. Value has been created. Every sale makes the world a little bit better for your customer.

Have this mindset when doing validation of any sort: "I'm here to bring value to these customers—and they will readily tell me how I can do that because it is in their best interest." With that in mind, your focus, first and foremost, should actually be on the customers you, for some reason, don't manage to serve—the ones who say no to your proposition—because the ones who say yes are now already served. Value has been created. The universe is in balance.

Look to the ones who say no because they hold the key to your improvement. Remember, they want to buy, and you are doing something to prevent that. Find out what it is and fix it.

Before we get to the individual methods of validation—conceptual sense, interviews, surveys, and market validation—I want to stress the single best concept I have for extracting valuable insights out of any of these methods: listen to the quality of the "no." We looked at this briefly in the previous chapter. Now it's time to examine it in more detail to see how understanding what a customer means by saying no can help you get a lot more people saying yes.

LISTEN TO THE QUALITY OF THE NO

It's very easy to turn validation into a quantitative exercise. You can score "likelihood to buy" on a one-to-five Likert scale, measure price sensitivity in surveys, and—when launching the product—measure conversion rates, MRR per lead, average selling price, and so forth. All of this is valid and gives you a good indication of whether and how the market is reacting.

However, it tells you nothing about *why* the market is reacting like it is. To figure that out, you have to talk to the customers, and you'll find there is much more information to be had from customers who didn't buy. From a quantitative standpoint, they are simply a zero. No sale. But you are interested in direction for action—insight into what you should do to turn that zero into a one.

So seek out those who say no and ask them, "Why?" Then shut up and listen. Be genuinely curious. Listen for the quality of the no. Is it a rejection of the job you are proposing to solve? Of the structure of your packaging? Of your pricing model? Too expensive? Or is it simply poor communication on your part, and the customer didn't get it—whatever "it" was?

Start by determining if the no is caused by lack of demand or by too much friction in your model. Think of a rocket that needs to launch: is it weak propulsion or poor aerodynamics that is keeping it from getting into orbit? If it is unclear, it isn't friction causing the no—it's fuel, a lack of demand.

Remember, your customers want you to have good pricing, so they will tell you in no uncertain terms if your crappy model is keeping them from making a purchase that they actually really want to make! However, that same customer will get "wool-in-mouth syndrome" if the real issue with your product is that they just don't want it. Most customers are nice people; they don't want to hurt your feelings, which includes telling you, "I'm just not that into you."

If, for example, your customer says, "This is a really great product. I'm sure you will do very well with this in the market," you have just received what I call "the kiss of death." Because one thing is for certain: *that* customer isn't buying.

So listen to the quality of the no. What kind of a no is it? Is it a "demand no?" Or a "structure no?" Or an "I-didn't-understand-what-you-just-said-to-me-so-I'm-just-playing-along-to-be-nice no?"

Try to use your framework to identify the issue:

1. Bad capability? (e.g., the core solution is not good enough for the job to be done)

2. Bad fencing?

3. Bad packaging?

4. Bad pricing model?

5. Too expensive?

6. Poor communication of any/all of the above?

Generally, number one and six are the fuel or demand part of your equation. Numbers two to five are the friction parts. When listening for the quality of the no, try to identify what—from the list—your customers are saying no to.

The concept of the "quality of the no" can be used across the board in all forms of validation: conceptual sense, interviews, surveys, and market validation.

IT HAS TO MAKE SENSE

If your pricing doesn't make sense to you, it's unlikely to make sense to your customers. If you can't remember it easily, explain it easily, and easily place a new customer into your pricing model, it's probably not going to perform that well in the market. This, importantly, is not a question of simplicity. Pricing can be quite complex and still make sense—especially if it's built on good packaging and around jobs to be done.

This is trickier than it seems because you have to be radically uncompromising on this issue. If your pricing "sort of makes sense," it's probably not good enough. If your customers "should" or "ought to" understand and accept your pricing, it's probably not good enough.

Again, as always with pricing, if you follow the process and ensure your fences are in place first, then your packaging, then your pricing model, then your price points, you should be able to arrive at solid pricing. The danger is that you may not yet have a model that is good enough, so you talk yourself into accepting something subpar.

When I do advisory work for startups and enterprise tech companies, my acid test for "pricing that makes sense" is whether I can sense that both the VP of Product and the VP of Sales are equally excited about launching and testing new pricing. Because they have access to two very different sources of customer feedback, I know if we can create a model that seems to fit well with both these perspectives, we have something worth taking forward.

Again, don't compromise here. Sure, you might have five different objectives you want to reach with your pricing; maybe you want to discriminate between verticals, geographies, and customer size while also preventing customers from sharing logins between users and creating a recurring-revenue model around your services. Okay, fair enough, but if trying to achieve all that has led you to create a weird, convoluted pricing model, then it doesn't really matter if it solves all your nice objectives, because it will only solve them on paper—not out in the marketplace.

So be uncompromising. Does it make sense? It's a yes-no question. If it doesn't, change it. Loosen up some of your objectives if you must. They are less important than the overall viability and salability of your model in the market.

Sometimes, when I run pricing design sprints, we "save" one of the founders or key executives and keep them out of the design process. We want them to come in with fresh eyes and look at the overall model we're proposing to determine if it makes sense before we move on to further validation. Your sales team can also serve that function: if they can immediately see how they can "operate" the new model, they probably can.

HOW TO VALIDATE THROUGH CUSTOMER INTERVIEWS

I'll say it again, customers want you to have good pricing. They want to have a valuable product, and they want to pay for it in a way that makes sense to them and fits their budgets and business model.

Of course, they would prefer to pay less rather than more, but in my experience, most B2B customers are actually fine with reasonable pricing. So you absolutely can and should talk to customers about your pricing and seek validation of it before you launch it into the market.

I usually advise my clients to book three to five interviews, of about thirty to forty-five minutes each, with current or prospective customers. When booking the interviews, you should tell the clients something like the following:

We are working on a redesign of our product packaging and our pricing model. Naturally, we would like this to be an attractive offering in the market, so we would like to invite you to a forty-five-minute Zoom call to show you version 1.0 of our new product packaging and pricing and get your honest feedback. This is not a sales call, and we're not going to ask what you would be willing to pay—we are focused only on the model itself and how it fits with your business.

I then put together a five-to-twelve slide presentation with the following structure:

1. Company presentation (if you must)

2. The job you are trying to solve

3. The packaging of the product (including fencing)

4. The packaging plus pricing model

5. The packaging plus pricing model plus price points

6. The packaging plus pricing model plus the price points of add-ons, services, etc.

7. Any number of FAQ-type backup slides if you foresee certain tricky questions that might need attention (e.g., a visual showing a discount curve, information about how resellers are paid, the packaging for the fence that this customer is not part of, etc.)

The idea is to ensure you get feedback from the customer on the right structural level about your packaging and pricing.

If you just show them the whole shebang straight out of the gate, you can't separate the feedback you get because most customers will immediately focus on the price point. And if they don't like your "ten dollar per user per month" model, you will have a hard time telling if it's the ten dollars they don't like or the user per month. So you should show it in a staged approach, in the order in which you designed it: packaging first, then pricing model, and then price points.

At each step in this process, you show them your slide, give them a minute to take it in (don't talk), and then ask:

1. Does it make sense to you?

2. Do you see yourself fitting into this model? (e.g., "Which of these packages would be for you?" or "Does this pricing metric work for you?")

That's it. If you establish that they understand the model and that they have demand for it, that's enough. Take any other feedback they have and engage in a conversation with them. This should be run as a semi-structured interview.

And now to the kicker: if they answer a hard no to either of those two questions, you don't proceed to the next slide.

Let's say, for example, you've shown them your new packaging, and they got it straight away, really liked it, and could immediately place themselves into it (e.g., "We would definitely go for the 'Agency' tier, given all the automation features there"). But when you showed them the pricing model—a price per client project, say—the customer was suddenly not onboard and said things like, "How would you even define that? We have clients who have been with us for years, and sometimes we structure hundreds of projects for them, but really these are part of one larger campaign. Also, some projects we have are really huge, but others are very, very small—and some of the smaller ones we don't make any money on. They are just done to sell other projects." And so on.

If that is the feedback you get on your #ClientProject pricing metric, you really can't use the feedback this customer would give you on the price point related to that metric—because any price is going to be "polluted" by the fact that the structure isn't a good fit for the customer. If you get a stop like this, you thank them for the feedback and pull out the third question:

3. What should we do instead, then, to create a [packaging/ pricing model/price point] that you'd like?

Then, it is essential to listen as hard as you can. You can, however, challenge, gently, to understand the boundaries. For example, if the customer suggests a "per user" metric, you can say something like, "We thought about that, but didn't go with it because we were concerned you would then limit the use of the software to only a few of your employees instead of spreading it across your organization to create more value. Do you think that concern is unwarranted?" You listen carefully to gauge if you've correctly understood the customer's job to be done, value chain, budget structure, perception of fairness, unit economics, and so on. Because if your pricing isn't working, it's likely due to you not fully understanding one of those underlying factors.

Now, you are likely going to get a bit of pushback or challenge on the price points. That is only natural. What you are listening for is how the customer is parsing the price points. What are they comparing them to? Their internal unit economics in their own revenue model? Competitor price points? The pricing of other software? The price they are currently paying?

Remember, no price is in itself high or low. Price is always evaluated in relation to something else. The interesting thing for you is what that "something else" is. Your packaging and your pricing model should ensure an easy and immediate connection to the value created.

One clue that the customer is on board is they start calculating the price other customers would be paying, e.g., "We have 40 users, so at $500 + $20/user that is $1,300 a month. Hmm...and a five-person agency would be $600 a month. Okay, that makes sense." Nobody likes to be a fool, so if the customer approves of the price points of other customers across sizes and use cases, they are likely to approve of the pricing they will pay too.

If you get a clear "hell no," accept it and ask why and what to do instead. You've most likely missed something further up in the structure; you've miscalculated the unit economics; and your price per unit somehow, or—finally—you've not properly taken discounts into account and need to work on the pricing here.

Can you tell in an interview if your price points are too low? No. Sorry, but it's rare that a customer will tell you to straight-up raise prices. If you get absolutely zero pushback on price points, you could simply run another round of three to five interviews with double the prices. Is it a perfect measurement tool? No. Pretty crude, actually. But if you really don't understand your own value in your market, this can be a fast way to get into striking distance of something that is roughly right.

Remember, you are there in the interview, being charming and all-knowing about the product. And the customer you are interviewing is selected in some manner—probably because of your existing good relationship or their already-stated interest in buying. Or both. So the playing field is already tilted in your favor. That means if an interview like this doesn't land somewhere between "quite positive" and "very excited," you have work to do. Sure, any single customer can have a personality or one of those days where they just aren't excitable, but that is why you're doing three to five interviews.

If you don't come out of a round of customer interviews like this and feel elevated and pumped about your product and offering, chances are it's not going to have the product-market fit you're looking for. But, at least, you should have some clearer ideas about exactly what you need to fix to get the desired result the next time around.

HOW TO VALIDATE THROUGH SURVEYS

Surveys are great early in the design process when you are gauging preferences for features, pricing metrics, and so forth. That, in itself, should improve the quality of your packaging and pricing.

However, for ACVs above $1,000, I believe interviews are much better at validating new packaging and pricing than surveys. That's because you are really mostly looking for validation of the structure and the design rather than the individual features or the price points themselves, which can be optimized later. But for smaller ACVs—or if you are in a hurry—conducting your validation through a survey can be useful.

Basically, you do it by creating a survey version of the validation interview using SurveyMonkey or a similar tool. I recommend structuring the survey across pages or sections as follows:

- Introduction email to get the respondent to do the survey— something like the invitation text in the previous section.

- Survey page 1: a general, short introduction to your company.

- Survey page 2: a short description of the job you are trying to do for your customers (e.g., automate banner ads, help designers reuse work, reduce risk in insurance workflows, etc.).

- Survey page 3: a visual representation of your packaging. Ask the customer to choose one (or several if you have modules) and provide a long-form text field where they can explain their thinking.

- Survey page 4: packaging again, this time with a pricing model included (e.g., price per user per month—billed per five users). Ask, "Do you think it's a fair model?" "Does this way of paying make sense in terms of how you'd use this software and how your budgets work?" "Do you have a suggestion for an even better model for us?" The answers to all these questions should be given in long-form text fields.

- Survey page 5: same as the previous page, except this time with price points (e.g., fifty dollars per user per month—billed per five users). Ask, "Do you think this pricing is fair?" Again, the space for answers should be long-form text fields.

- The end.

Some would argue that you can use page 5 to optimize prices by asking some form of a price sensitivity question. You can, but if you do that, you are not validating; you are optimizing. Of course, there's no harm in that. In fact, for low ACVs, it can be a great opportunity to do either a Van Westendorp or a Gabor Granger (Google is your friend). For higher ACVs, broad-brush, price-sensitivity surveys are pretty worthless (but anyway, you are more likely to be doing interviews, right?).

Also, don't get too hung up on the price point. The perfect outcome is that you've designed an offering your customers actually want. They like your packaging. They think your pricing model makes sense. They think your price points are acceptable. Perfect. Now, you can move forward. Remember, a good plan executed today is far superior to a perfect plan executed tomorrow.

HOW TO VALIDATE THROUGH SALES

MARKET TESTING

The gold standard of validation is, of course, actually getting customers to buy. Regardless of what other forms of validation you'll do—or not do—you'll end up having to actually proposition new customers with your new packaging and pricing sooner or later.

Until you actually push your new offering into the market, you simply cannot be certain that it will work. You can have a model that makes total sense on paper. The surveys give clear direction. The customer interviews went really great. And then, when you go live, you hit a snag. You missed something. Thirty percent of customers want—really want—a feature moved from one package to another. The pricing is actually hard for your reps to explain, so customers zone out. And so on.

So market testing is both unavoidable and necessary. When it works, it's like hitting half a mile of all green lights at full speed through a city. When you start realizing this is actually going to work, you're ecstatic.

The weakness of market testing, however, is that anything short of total success and all green lights is really hard to unpack. If it isn't working, it's not always immediately clear why. Why do the customers want that feature moved? Did you not understand their job to be done well enough? Did you miss an obvious fencing opportunity? And why is the pricing hard to explain? Did you misunderstand the customer's value chain or their budget structure? Are your reps just not used to this new, higher ACV?

Market testing validates the whole, combined proposition of product and pricing as they are being executed in your customer-acquisition model. But just as it is hard to predict the interplay of all these moving parts in your new commercial model before the launch, it is equally hard to then pinpoint what parts of the process are at fault if the mojo just isn't there.

Even worse, you actually don't know what a good result should look like because what is your baseline? Your old model? You should obviously aim to do better than that, but how much better? And even if you do considerably better, you might miss an opportunity to improve even more because you can't see all the shortcomings for all the apparent success.

It's so exhilarating to drive 50 mph through all green lights that you never consider whether you could have gone 80 mph!

A case in point, in 2018, when I first worked with Contractbook. com, I raised its average selling price by 1,000 percent. That was great, of course. But less than a year later, we raised it by another 70 percent and reworked major parts of the model. Most companies wouldn't have done that; they would have just settled for the first rework, which created a "good enough" model for them to grow.

This is where the quality of the no comes in. Listening to and understanding those customers who aren't buying helps you to drive even more growth. But validation via market testing is different from surveys and interviews in that it's probably your sales reps and not your product team who have to do the listening. And they have to do that *while* trying to sell the product.

Align with your sales leadership before you launch new pricing, stressing that while it is, of course, important to sell, the sales team also has an important role in extracting feedback from customers and funneling it back to Product and Pricing.

The concept of the "quality of the no" usually resonates with Sales. Did the customer not like the product because:

1. No demand

—or any combination of the below—

2. Packaging not right

3. Pricing model not right

4. Too expensive

Have sales reps identify the reason for any lost sales and then review that data weekly together with Sales management to answer the question, "Why are the customers saying no?" Be prepared for sales reps to always blame price points, but don't accept that straight away. Instead turn the conversation around by saying, "What could we do on the core value of the product, the packaging, and the model to reduce the need for discounts or a lower price?" Remind the sales reps that they're the ones who talk to customers all day, so they need to have a perspective on this and send it back to Product if they ever want to have something better to sell.

Then have Pricing and Product debrief with Sales on a weekly basis to understand what is going on. If you want a faster turnaround time on the learning, you can also have team members from Product or Pricing listen in to sales calls and then discuss items one through four with sales reps after each call.

This is all good if you have live sales reps talking to customers, but if you have self-service sales, you have to work around the fact that you don't have a built-in opportunity to talk to customers and listen to the quality of the no. Your best option here is to conduct solid surveys prior to launch or—if you can't do such surveys prelaunch due to time constraints or other factors—run the validation survey in parallel with launching the new pricing, and pay special attention to the customers who don't buy.

You can also simply call up a few lost sales customers and run a postmortem on their rejection of your product (e.g., if they churned after a free trial, etc.) using a structure similar to the validation interview. (But expect to only get five to fifteen minutes of their time, so move fast.)

All of this "quality of no" stuff doesn't mean you should not hit your numbers or measure every reasonable KPI of your sales process. Those things need to happen too. You just have to realize that while the quantitative measurements might tell you that something needs fixing, it's the qualitative stuff that tells you how to fix it.

Next, it's time to explore how correctly applied and structured discounts can be a powerful tool to secure and retain customers, which is the subject of Chapter 8.

EIGHT

DISCOUNTS

DISCOUNTS ARE A PROFIT TOOL

Discounts are generally dismissed and disliked. Pick any ten books on pricing, and you'll find the authors competing to see who can show the most disdain for discounts. If Sales can't sell without giving discounts, that just proves they lack discipline and skill. They should be blamed for failing to communicate the product's value. After all, if you sell for 10 percent less, you make 10 percent less money!

Sure.

If you want to hear the other side of this argument, try speaking with the salespeople themselves, the people who are out there doing the job and trying to meet quarterly or monthly sales quotas. They do this by talking to customers—many of whom expect discounts!

Discounts are a powerful tool, and for that reason, they can be powerfully misused. Good discounting can be achieved, however, when you reduce prices for some customers, some of the time, for some good reason. If you reduce prices for all customers, all of the time, for any old reason, you are probably aware you have a problem.

There are generally two types of discounts you should focus on getting right:

1. Structural discounts

2. Sales discounts

We will cover a third kind—post-sales discounts—later, but that is a minor issue compared to the other two.

Let's start by taking a look at this oversimplified visualization, which shows the relationship between customers' willingness to pay and pricing, as well as how that changes as the amount they purchase increases:

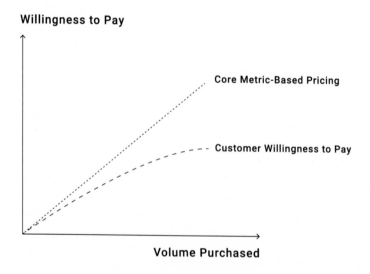

Figure 58: For most markets, the willingness to pay doesn't increase in a linear format with the volume purchased but tapers off as the customers use their buying power to demand better unit prices at higher volumes.

The general rule is that the more volume the customer is purchasing, the better the unit price they will expect. So if one unit equals $100, then one million units will very rarely equals $100M.

This is a statistical concept in the sense that at any given price there is a percent likelihood that a customer is going to buy. So say you have a 30 percent conversion rate at one unit = $100, then we want to know at what dollar amount per unit we can maintain that 30 percent conversion rate when the #Units goes up.

The problem is that it is really hard to tell. Large volumes of units, by definition, mean large customers, which means that you aren't going to have that many of them, and the likelihood that each one has its own particular circumstances is pretty high. So it's hard to run any kind of meaningful statistical analysis.

That is where sales discounts come in as a potential solution. The argument is that salespeople will just have to judge on a customer-by-customer basis what each case can carry in terms of pricing and then issue discounts to fit.

Schematically, that looks something like this:

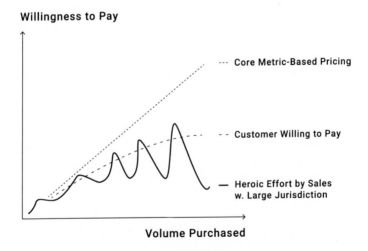

Figure 59: Sales' ability to properly access the real willingness to pay of larger customers is almost always subject to large variability. As a result, the actually executed prices are all over the place, created on a case-by-case basis.

There are several issues with this.

Due to commission structures, the loss of a sale means far more to the individual sales rep than it does to the business as a whole. If you have long sales cycles (and high ACVs to match), your sales rep is heavily personally invested in the sale. So for them, it makes total sense to err on the side of lower prices.

You face a similar situation with your real estate broker. He will tell you his incentive is aligned with yours when he takes a 2 percent commission to sell your house. You sell for $1M; he makes $20K. But when he has a potential buyer interested, he will already have done 90 percent of the work required for a sale. If the buyer wants a 10 percent discount, taking your $1M down to $900K, that only means a reduction in commission from $20K to $18K. The alternative—for the broker—is to write off the work and time already invested and go in search of a new buyer. If he does that, he might be able to sell the same house for a higher price, potentially making somewhere between $1K and $2K extra in commission for all that additional effort. Clearly, that doesn't make sense, so the broker now leans on you to accept the $900K offer. But if you have an $800K mortgage on the house, that means losing 50 percent of your profits.

Based on that same principle, your worst sales reps can cost you fortunes in discounts, and often the best decision is to simply not let them anywhere near customers.

These issues become even tougher when the sales become larger. If your standard volume is, say, five-user sales at $100 per user, then it's pretty clear to most people that if we're giving discounts, they are going to be pretty small. But what if a customer with 10,000 users comes along? Now we break out the big numbers. I've seen volume discounts go as high as 98.5 percent!

If it's not immediately clear if the discount should be 50 percent, 60 percent, or 70 percent because of sheer volume, you are still talking about a huge range of potential price levels being executed. Enter structural discounts.

Willingness to Pay

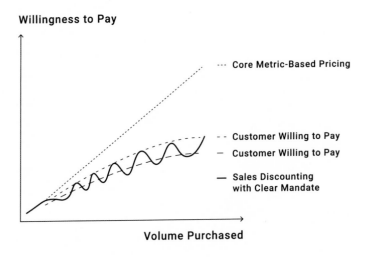

··· Core Metric-Based Pricing

– – Customer Willing to Pay

— Customer Willing to Pay

— Sales Discounting with Clear Mandate

Volume Purchased

Figure 60: With a structural discount in place that generates pricing more appropriate to the customers' real willingness to pay as volumes increase, the sales team only has to apply small sales discounts to close the customer, if any at all. This creates much more consistency in executed prices across customers.

Structural discounts are simply predetermined discounts that are often openly shown to customers in negotiations. They work to preempt the majority of the discount needed for higher volume sales, which in turn reduces the need for sales discounts.

For example, maybe users 1 to 100 cost $100/month each, but the price then drops to $80 for user numbers between 101 and 250. And it falls further to $60 when the user numbers go above 251. As these discounts are both predetermined and transparent, we can describe them as structural.

There is a larger point behind this: discounts should not be owned by Sales. Discounts should be owned by either Senior Management or a designated Pricing Function in the organization, both of which have the economics of the product as a whole in mind.

The centralization of discounting—just like the centralization of pricing and packaging—forces you to create a joint understanding of the offering you are taking to market across Sales, Product, Marketing, and Senior Management. The economic unit now is the product (which can scale) and not the customer (which can't).

Structural discounts are determined centrally across these functions, and so are the mandates and standard operating procedures that govern the use of sales discounts. This also takes the pressure off the individual sales rep. If she knows she can only give a 10 percent discount and only to customers with more than one hundred users, she will try to work the sale of sub-one hundred-user customers differently. If the sale is then lost because of price sensitivity, that will be the responsibility of Sales management and the Pricing Function who laid out the discount structure—not the sales rep.

Now that we've introduced structural and sales discounts, let's go over the design and operationalization of both in the following sections.

STRUCTURAL DISCOUNTS

Structural discounts are a price-discrimination tool. The tool's core function—in combination with your pricing model—is to allow you to charge different prices to different customers.

That is both simple and powerful.

Generally, structural discounts should be applied to the core value metric while allowing any other elements of your pricing architecture to be relatively untouched. Chapter 5 on Wallet Structuring gives more detail about designing the revenue mix and tapping into different customer budgets—but that often happens against a backdrop of discounting on the core pricing metric.

So if you are pricing your core metric per #MonthlyActiveUser and want to create a structure where discounts are applied as certain volumes are reached, that doesn't mean you should also discount your add-ons, such as Premium SLAs or the like.

Take a look at this customer example of a structural discount:

HARDWARE UNIT
36 months of
battery guarantee

$30/PCS

LICENSE

What you get:

- All core Bluetooth use cases
- Access to global network
- Rule creation on machine level

$3.50/MONTH

Licenses	250	1,000	2,500	5,000	10,000	25,000	50,000	100,000	200,000	300,000	400,000
Discount	0%	10%	20%	30%	40%	50%	60%	70%	80%	85%	87.5%

Figure 61: Example of a structural discount spanning a very large range of different volumes—from a few hundred to nearly half a million units. Notice that the lower-margin hardware units have a stable price at all volumes, while the high-margin SaaS license has a very wide discount margin.

In this example, we are selling Bluetooth tags in a construction IoT setting, so it's a combination of hardware and software. The hardware is $30 a piece, with a $3.50 monthly license attached. However, as more licenses are purchased, this price goes down significantly, creating this scenario for the customer:

MODEL

DISCOUNT GOES TO 87.5%
BASE LICENSE PRICE $3.50

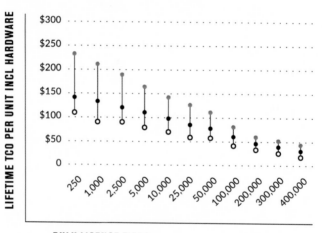

Figure 62: The pricing model from Figure 61 now laid out as a total cost of ownership (TCO) calculation across different volumes. Notice how the discount curve flattens out at the end, generating incrementally fewer discounts at super-high volumes.

As you can see, the total cost of ownership per unit drops drastically as volume increases through the tiers. This is, of course, intentional. The IoT vendor has a decent number of smaller customers who only have use cases for a few hundred or a few thousand units.

The majority of customers, however, are large, national construction companies with the potential for totals of 5,000 to 20,000 units. These customers turn over billions of dollars a year and are used to getting discounts based on their size. In their own minds, they are "big" and have lots of negotiation power.

The very largest customers of this IoT vendor are the super-large, global OEMs in the construction space (like Caterpillar, Manitou, and DeWalt), and such customers could easily have hundreds of thousands of units globally.

If pricing and discounts were up to individual sales reps, you would have an extremely large variance of prices across multiple customers, which is actually what the previous pricing model helped to clean up. Instead, with a fixed, structurally determined discount structure, each sales rep now has a predefined "discount slope" or rate of price changes related to volume. That prevents 70 percent discounts from being applied to twenty-five thousand unit cases and eroding profitability.

A reasonable internal discussion among senior sales reps should enable you to create an initial, overall discount slope. Simply ask yourselves what reasonable pricing looks like for varying sizes of customers and input that in a price/volume matrix. Then draw the approximate discount curve. You can also add about 10–20 percent to this pricing if you want to allow your reps to work with sales discounts as well.

WATERFALL OR THRESHOLD DISCOUNTS?

If the customer reaches a new volume tranche, should you then apply the discounted price to all units the customer has? If you do, then you are using a threshold model, where the discount is universally applied once the customer passes through a certain threshold. The alternative is to only apply the discount to those units above a certain volume, creating a "waterfall model" where the first units have a higher price than the last units.

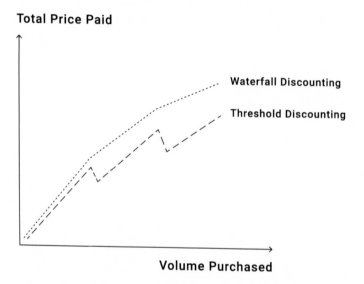

Total Price Paid

Waterfall Discounting

Threshold Discounting

Volume Purchased

Figure 63: Waterfall discounts apply a discount only to units above a certain number, while threshold discounts apply the discount to all units once that threshold is reached. The latter is good at incentivizing the customer to reach certain volumes.

One of the benefits of a threshold model is simplicity. Every unit has the same price, which makes it easier to communicate and explain, all else being equal. One of the dynamics, however, of a threshold model is that the net price actually drops once a new threshold is reached. This can create a situation where—for example—it is actually more expensive to buy eighty units than it is to buy one hundred.

If applied to the right scenario, this is a feature, not a bug. Precisely because larger volumes can be net cheaper for the customer once thresholds are reached, threshold models are well suited to discounting in scenarios where the volume is actually controlled by the customer (e.g., number of users or number of locations).

However, if it's not a metric the customer has control over, such as visits to a website or some other metric that is controlled by the behavior of your customers' customers, then there is no behavior you can affect. The customer will now simply be annoyed that they could pay net less if only they had a little more volume.

So threshold dynamics are good if you want to drive adoption and volume expansion in your accounts. If that is not the case, you should go for waterfall dynamics.

MAKE THE STRUCTURE BIGGER THAN YOUR CUSTOMERS

One mistake I often see with structural discounts, and price lists generally, is that they are not big enough. Take this example:

GMV Gross Merchant Value	<$10K	<$25K	<$75K	<$150K	<$500K	<$1M	<$2.5M
Commission	10%	9%	8%	7%	6%	5%	4%

Figure 64: Example discount structure of a pricing based off of a percentage of gross merchant value between $0 and $2.5M GMV.

Here, we are selling restaurant software that takes a commission of the gross merchant value (GMV)—i.e., revenue—that passes through our system. If less than $10,000 passes through in a month, we charge 10 percent of that volume. If between $1 million and $2.5 million passes through, we charge 4 percent.

But what happens when a chain restaurant with ten locations and $25 million in turnover calls? Well, then you negotiate. Here, your own discount structure has put you at a disadvantage because your customer will take the implied discount slope in your structure and try to extrapolate that out to their size. Which, in this case, would produce a figure that is less than zero percent. So the customer's psychological starting point is that the commission has to be very, very low.

Now, imagine you had presented them with this structure instead:

GMV Gross Merchant Value	<$10K	<$25K	<$75K	<$150K	<$500K	<$1M	<$2.5M	<$105M	<$50M	<$100M
Commission	10%	9%	8%	7%	6%	5%	4%	3.8%	3.7%	3.65%

Figure 65: Same discount structure but now extended to $100M GMV.

First of all, the big customer can now place themselves in your discount structure. They know that you've anticipated a customer of their size and how you've priced their volume. So far, so good.

But what's really good about this is they can also see how you have priced customers that are up to four times larger than them. That levels the playing field during negotiations. If a customer feels like they are the most important lead that ever walked through your door, they are going to want to get paid for that. Don't allow this. Always build your pricing structure big enough so that your largest potential customer would only be about two-thirds into the model.

Finally, by creating pricing for customers larger than the one with whom you are currently negotiating, you've already set the scene for the type of negotiation you are going to have.

The $25M GMV customer can read in the structure that you are willing to give them a 3.7 percent commission rate. That is great. But you've also stated that to get 3.65 percent they would need to show up with $100M in GMV, which, of course, they can't. This tends to put the brakes on the aggressiveness of the purchasing department you are negotiating with.

The final tweak to employ here is to let your discount slope flatten out at some point. In the previous example, we see it drop steadily in 1 percent increments from 10 percent to 4 percent, but then it suddenly seems like you get much stingier with further discounts as the rate now drops by just 0.2, 0.1, and 0.05 percent in the next three steps.

Your customer's natural interpretation will be that you are somehow drawing an invisible line in the sand. Stating directly in your pricing structure that there is a price point below which you are just not going to offer discounts—regardless of the size of the opportunity.

Often, the implicit assumption will be that you have some sort of cost dynamics at play that simply puts a limit on the pricing at which you can remain profitable. And that signaling is one of the great benefits of structural discounts. If they are designed right, they provide a negotiation framework around your pricing discussion that allows you to defend your pricing much better—further reducing the need for sales discounts.

One of the key tenets of negotiation is that your counterpart is not going to accept an agreement if they think there is still a better deal to be had. The psychology behind this is that we're hardwired to try and avoid regret. If you bargain for a house and push the price down from $1M to $955K, you might be pretty pleased with yourself until you learn that the seller was willing to part with it for $800K! The sheer regret of having "overpaid" might make that house almost uninhabitable for you!

In almost all cases, customers don't bargain to get a better price. They bargain to make sure they've got the best price there is. The difference is key. Only very rarely do you have a situation where you are selling to a sophisticated customer who is doing a real price-and-value comparison across vendors. In that situation, price actually matters. But, unless your offering is heavily commoditized, even in that situation bargaining by customers is mostly regret insurance.

SALES DISCOUNTS

Sales discounts mainly function as a communication tool to let the customer know that they have the best deal possible and will not regret buying at this price. This means that discounts, when given at all, should be given only reluctantly. Otherwise, they don't provide the customer with the feeling that they have now reached the limit and no further discounts can be given.

Imagine being in a bazaar, bargaining for a Persian rug. The merchant is wailing and crying with each discount he gives you, shifting from threats to pleas for mercy. This is great customer service. Because when you finally leave with your new rug, you do so feeling certain that you really got a great deal—even if you actually paid ten times as much as any local would have!

If the merchant had just given you the discount, dispassionately, you would not think this was really, truly, the best price to be had. So you might have pressed harder for more discounts or—not feeling comfortable with the situation—have moved on, postponing the decision to later.

Again, sales discounts are a communication tool, and as with any communication, the delivery matters more than the message. For that reason, the size and nature of the sales discount matter less than you would imagine, which means you should definitely use the ones that are most beneficial to you financially.

You should also always only offer discounts in a *quid pro quo* format, where you ask for something in return for the discount. For example, you could insist the customer makes annual payments instead of monthly or that they sign before the end of the quarter—whatever works for you.

Bearing all that in mind, let's look at the different types of sales discounts and the order of priority that you should put them in.

TYPES AND PRIORITIZATION OF SALES DISCOUNTS

Essentially, there are five types of sales discounts. I usually advise my clients to offer them in the following order of priority, starting with the most preferred type at the top.

1. Time-Limited, Short Duration

The most preferred type of sales discount should be time limited and only available for a short duration, such as "first three months free." This is especially good for small and medium-sized ACVs that are under $25K—generally the type of product where you would be on a monthly payment plan. For larger ACVs, it would usually translate to a discount for the first calendar year but probably not 100 percent off.

The benefit of the time-limited discount, besides actually helping to close customers, is that it leaves your run-rate ARR growth completely unscathed. If you sell a $10K ACV product with the first six months free, you still get to write up your ARR with the full $10K. This is, of course, only valuable if you are seeking funding or are a listed company.

2. Time-Limited, Long Duration

This means extending the time-limited discount for longer works as a compromise between full-on permanent discounts and no discounting at all. Obviously, a 20 percent discount for the next three years is definitely better for you than a permanent 20 percent discount.

That is both because you actually get to raise prices in three years (duh) and because it allows you to continuously "roll up" your customers to whatever current pricing you have, which is easier for you to handle operationally. Much more on that in the next chapter: "Raising Prices."

An aggressive version of time-limited, long discounts involves offering very large, very long discounts in a staged manner (e.g., 90 percent first year, 80 percent second year, 70 percent third year). This can turn out really well for you, especially if you have a very sticky product and you have the funding to wait out the first few years.

3. Terms and Conditions

Another form of sales discounts is to offer better terms and conditions. This can include better payment terms, better cancellation terms, guarantees of no price increases for three years, and so on. Just make sure to have a specifically defined list of terms and conditions that can be given, so that your sales reps don't get creative and draw up unique contracts for every customer.

Even though this is technically free, it's not on the top of the list of sales discounts, as my experience is that handling varying contracts creates a certain operational "load." But if you have large ACVs above $100K and are by and large drawing up new contracts for every new customer, then using T&Cs as negotiation leverage before giving up ARR is definitely a good strategy.

4. Upsell with a Permanent Discount

If you can't offer a time-limited discount in some form or close the customer with better terms, then the last line of defense before you offer an outright discount on the purchase is to try and simply offer more of the product instead.

For example, imagine you have three tiers at $499, $899, and $1,299 per month, and the customer wants a better price on the middle tier. You would be better off if you can close that customer on $899 by offering the top tier, rather than closing on the second tier at a price of, say, $799. (This, of course, assumes that your costs are negligible—adjust appropriately.)

This can also be combined with a time limit. Ask the customer to pay the full second-tier price of $899 but offer to give them access to the third-tier for the next two years. If you are lucky, the customer will upgrade to the full $1,299 in a couple of years once they have properly adopted the product.

5. Permanent Discount on Preferred Product

Finally, of course, you can also give a straight-up, permanent price reduction on the product preferred by the customer. The most common version of this is "pay annually and get two months free," which is fine, except I have never once seen "pay annually and get two months free" outperform "pay annually and get a 5 percent discount." Again, it's rarely the amount that matters. Remember that sales discounts are a communication tool, allowing you to let the customer know they have the best deal they can get.

There are a few other tips and tricks for reducing the load of permanent discounts. One is to offer them in small increments. Don't be lazy and just offer a 10 percent discount; offer a 4 percent discount. Then 6 percent. You will be surprised how such a small change can reduce the average percentage discount of your sales.

Offer discounts in nominal amounts, not in percentages—at least in terms of what you put in the contract. So if you want to offer a 15 percent discount on an $899 package, don't write "a 15 percent discount" in the contract; write "$134 discount." Because then, when you raise the list price of your product from $899 to $999, your original discount doesn't apply to the $100 price increase. So if you raise prices 10 percent a year for ten years, a nominal discount will be reduced to an effective 3.8 percent instead of the full 10 percent.

SALES' STANDARD OPERATING PROCEDURES

Your sales reps will only use the discounts you allow them to use. So the most straightforward way to control discounts is to create standard operating procedures (SOPs) that determine who gets to use what discounts when.

The most basic form is escalation: above a certain level of discount, the rep has to go to Sales leadership for approval. I usually create extra obstacles to this, especially at very large discount levels, by stating in the SOPs that certain discounts can only be given by two executives in conjunction. This is like the two sets of keys needed to launch a nuclear weapon: the rule is there to ensure the missile is never actually fired. Learn from that.

The SOPs and escalation ladder can work on both a type and a size axis (e.g., all reps can offer time-limited, short discounts of up to "three months half price," but longer or higher discounts need to be escalated for approval). Make the SOPs as simple as possible, bearing in mind that their primary function is to get the rep to focus on selling the product rather than focusing on what discount to pull out of the hat next.

PRICE DISCOVERY

Finally, sales discounts have one application where they are not solely a communication tool to let the customer know they have the best available deal: when you don't actually know what to charge. For example, when you first go upmarket with your product, you may now be dealing with customers of a size that you have not previously encountered. And since you don't know their price sensitivity, it can be really hard for you to establish a structural discount slope that is roughly right.

In a case like that, sales discounts can be used in a "price discovery" phase. That basically means for a short period of time and with a clear SOP for their use, sales discounts can be quite large—say, up to 50 percent on the permanent ARR.

The point of this phase is to sell to these customers but to give discounts as reluctantly as possible. You can then look at actual executed prices and draw up a structural discount slope to reduce the use of sales discounts.

This is, *de facto*, what often happens when you have to launch your new enterprise software using a handful of pilot customers: each and every one of them gets a bespoke contract with special terms. After a year and a half, when you've sold a couple dozen of these, you can look back and start to gauge which ones were "good deals" and which ones you closed too low. You then use this hard-earned experience to draw up a firmer pricing structure, with structural discounts, and reduce the mandate for giving sales discounts accordingly.

POST-SALES DISCOUNTS

One special type of discounting remains to be discussed: the discounts you offer to customers who you've already closed. These post-sales discounts are used to prevent churn, and they can be done either by "grandfathering," being proactive, or being reactive. Let's look at each of those methods in turn.

GRANDFATHERING

Grandfathering is the practice of not raising prices for some or all of your existing customers, even though your list prices overall are increasing.

Maybe you've recently raised prices for this group of customers. Maybe you feel like you owe them a debt of loyalty (I hear this a lot. You don't). But the most common scenario is simply a fear of undue churn if prices are raised, causing a drop in ARR ahead of some important funding round or similar event.

Grandfathering is fine overall but keep it in proportion. Imagine you just raised prices by 40 percent for all new customers after diligent market testing. Not grandfathering your current customers would have to result in 30 percent churn or more in order for you to be better off grandfathering those customers.

The prioritized list of sales discount types given in the previous section applies here too. It's better to announce a time-limited grandfathering of, say, one year, rather than a permanent one. Or raise prices but guarantee no more price increases for the next three years (a terms discount).

But, by and large, the squeeze isn't worth the juice with grand-fathering. That's partly because you are likely to overestimate the churn risk. It's also because, even if you see the increase in ARR due to higher pricing eroded away by churn, the simple fact that rolling over legacy customers to your new pricing saves you the extra operational load of dealing with multiple pricing cohorts and makes it a preferred scenario.

So generally, I advise that the best ARR scenario is cherry-picking the largest and most sensitive customers for grandfathering while just rolling up the rest of the legacy cohorts.

PROACTIVE PRICE REDUCTION

In rare instances, you can offer to lower existing customers' prices, either temporarily or permanently. That is most often done to buy a customer's patience, either because your promised and much-advertised roadmap is significantly delayed, or because you somehow messed something up and need to make amends.

For example, I once had a large insurtech client who offered all of its customers a reduced price for a year following a major security breach in one of their data centers. This breach had threatened to build a consensus among the customers to find another provider.

Another version of a proactive price reduction is to offer parts of a product for free, for a period of time, if you can see that the customer hasn't properly adopted it yet and maybe regrets buying it as a result. The free period can effectively "reset the clock" and rejuvenate the customer's perception of their product and their enthusiasm to adopt it.

Usually, such cases are handled by Customer Success in coordination with Management, or by the direct account manager.

REACTIVE PRICE REDUCTION

Sometimes, you lower prices simply because your existing customers want you to.

The normal scenario in such cases is an annual "price review," where your customer's procurement department has decided they would like to reduce all costs by 4 percent. This has to be stopped at the contract level, and you should generally never accept a scenario where you continuously have to accept periodic renegotiations; they will never be in your favor. You want your contract to create a firm ultimatum: the prices are what they are, and if the customer doesn't like them, they can leave.

That said, sometimes the customer will ask anyway. If you, for some reason, feel it is warranted, be reasonable and follow the five-point prioritized list from the previous section: time-limited discounts for short durations first, then for longer, and so on. I'd say this has to be reserved for special occasions only, and usually only for those cases where you would actually have been fine offering a proactive price reduction.

The other scenario for reactive price reduction is last-minute churn prevention: if the customer calls in to churn, or in any other way announces they want to leave, you can offer a discount in exchange for them staying on. The most effective scenario here is, again, if the customer churns due to a lack of adoption. Offer to "reset the clock" by giving a free period, and then redouble your efforts to make the customer adopt the product.

If the customer actually has a genuine issue with the product for some reason, then discounts are unlikely to really do any good. Sure, you might retain a bit of ARR for a while, but the whole operational side of juggling unsatisfied customers, who are actually committed to leaving, is likely not the best use of your time.

Now that we've thoroughly examined discounting, it's time to turn to the flip side of that particular coin: raising prices. Chapter 9 explains why it is necessary to regularly raise the price of SaaS products to match their increasing value and how this can be achieved with minimal churn.

NINE

RAISING PRICES

HYDRAS AND MONOLITHS: HOW NOT TO RAISE PRICES

If you've followed all the advice in the previous chapters, you've hopefully, through much hard work, blood, sweat, and tears, finally created a pricing structure that works for you and your customers—who are now happily set up on their various tiers and contented with the price they're paying.

Now, it's time to raise that price.

Of course, I'm not recommending instantaneous price rises as soon as you've got a customer settled, but price rises certainly should happen pretty frequently. You should probably raise your prices at least annually, if not quarterly.

Here is why: you are selling a SaaS product. That implies you are going to keep developing the software over time, not only ensuring the continued function of existing use cases but also improving them and adding new functionality to power new use cases.

In other words, if a customer signs with you today for a perpetually recurring contract, you have no idea what product you will be selling that customer a year from now. And, consequently, that customer has no idea what they will be buying from you. So how can you agree what the future price should be?

You can't. Or at least, you shouldn't. So you set a price for what they are buying today when they are buying it. And then you raise it later when the product has changed and—presumably—increased in value to that customer.

Contractually fixing prices indefinitely into the future with no easy mechanism to raise or update them without triggering a renegotiation is one of the most common mistakes I see B2B SaaS companies make. And it is a mistake that is not fixable with a simple, predetermined annual price adjustment—e.g., +4 percent every year (I usually see them ranging from 2 percent to 7 percent in practice, 4 percent to 5 percent being the norm).

Again, you really, truly, do not know what you will be selling your customers in the future. How do you, then, know that it's going to be 4 percent more valuable?

Also, in most contracts I see, the fixed annual percentage price increase seems to be inserted instead of an inflation adjustment clause—sometimes in the format "4 percent or inflation, whichever is higher." Okay, but what if inflation is 4 percent (not a stretch of the imagination here in mid-2022), but your product increases 15 percent in value to your customers due to the brilliant new functionality your teams roll out?

Take a look at this table:

Year	Price Not Adjusted	Fixed Price Increase	Price Fixed Adjustment	Inflation	Price Inflation Adjustment	% Value Increase of Product	Price Fully Adjusted
2022	100 USD	4%	100 USD	3%	100 USD	6%	100 USD
2023	100 USD	4%	104 USD	2%	103 USD	8%	109 USD
2024	100 USD	4%	108 USD	0%	105 USD	15%	120 USD
2025	100 USD	4%	112 USD	4%	105 USD	-4%	138 USD
2026	100 USD	4%	117 USD	3%	109 USD	11%	138 USD
Total CLV	500 USD		542 USD		522 USD		605 USD
CLV Index	100%		108%		104%		121%
Price Index	100%		117%		109%		138%

Figure 66: Price adjustment scenarios based on fixed, inflation, or value-based pricing. Note that value-based adds inflation as well, as you want to increase the price of your product in real terms in accordance with the actual increase in product value to the customer.

If you sell something at $100 (or index = 100) and don't change prices for five years, then you are still going to charge those same $100 from that same customer five years later. If that is you, comfort yourself with the fact that you are in good company. More than half of all B2B SaaS businesses do this, relying only on product upselling and metric expansion to power ARPA increases.

As price adjustments happen at the end of a period, and we have four year-ends to adjust in the previous scenario; your 4 percent annual adjustment will compound to a total of a +17 percent price increase in the fifth year. An inflation scenario is, of course, way more unpredictable but would average about 2 percent in the past couple of decades.

What is even more unpredictable than inflation is the value increase or decrease of your offering to your market. In the previous table, I've used some relatively *conservative* numbers. If you are a startup, you may agree that it isn't out of the ordinary to add significant product value year on year to the tune of +20–50 percent.

So even with the conservative product value increases, which might better fit a $50M–250M ARR enterprise, we can see that the impact on price over time is massive compared to small, fixed increases. Importantly, this differs on a CLV basis (which accumulates) as compared to a price-index base (which compounds) because it's the price index that will determine your future CLV and, hence, the valuation of your company.

EFFECTS OF QUARTERLY PRICE CHANGES

Maybe you're wondering what would happen if we ran the same scenario, but instead of changing prices annually, we change them quarterly? Here is a breakdown, assuming the $100 is paid in $25 quarterly portions, and all percentage increases portion out to compound to the same end number (e.g., we've taken into account that 1 percent a quarter compounds faster than 4 percent a year and adjusted quarterly percentages accordingly).

The impact is actually massive and even bigger for larger percentage product value increases. If you are raising venture capital at the end of Q4 2026, you will have a +13.7 percent higher executed price to raise from in the quarterly scenario, which, from a valuation perspective, might pay for that entire funding round.

YEAR	PRICE - Not Adjusted	FIXED PRICE INCREASE	PRICE - Fixed Adjustment	INFLATION	PRICE - Inflation Adjusted	% VALUE INCREASE OF PRODUCT	PRICE - Fully Adjusted
2022-Q1	25 USD	0.985%	25 USD	0.742%	25 USD	1.467%	25 USD
2022-Q2	25 USD	0.985%	25 USD	0.742%	25 USD	1.467%	26 USD
2022-Q3	25 USD	0.985%	26 USD	0.742%	26 USD	1.467%	26 USD
2022-Q4	25 USD	0.985%	26 USD	0.742%	26 USD	1.467%	27 USD
2023-Q1	25 USD	0.985%	26 USD	.0.496%	26 USD	1.943%	27 USD
2023-Q2	25 USD	0.985%	27 USD	0.496%	26 USD	1.943%	28 USD
2023-Q3	25 USD	0.985%	27 USD	0.496%	26 USD	1.943%	29 USD
2023-Q4	25 USD	0.985%	27 USD	0.496%	26 USD	1.943%	29 USD
2024-Q1	25 USD	0.985%	27 USD	0.000%	26 USD	3.556%	30 USD
2024-Q2	25 USD	0.985%	28 USD	0.000%	26 USD	3.556%	31 USD
2024-Q3	25 USD	0.985%	28 USD	0.000%	26 USD	3.556%	32 USD
2024-Q4	25 USD	0.985%	28 USD	0.000%	26 USD	3.556%	33 USD
2025-Q1	25 USD	0.985%	28 USD	0.985%	26 USD	-0.251%	35 USD
2025-Q2	25 USD	0.985%	29 USD	0.985%	27 USD	-0.251%	35 USD
2025-Q3	25 USD	0.985%	29 USD	0.985%	27 USD	-0.251%	35 USD
2025-Q4	25 USD	0.985%	29 USD	0.985%	27 USD	-0.251%	35 USD
2026-Q1	25 USD	0.985%	30 USD	0.742%	28 USD	2.643%	36 USD
2026-Q2	25 USD	0.985%	30 USD	0.742%	28 USD	2.643%	37 USD
2026-Q3	25 USD	0.985%	30 USD	0.742%	28 USD	2.643%	38 USD
2026-Q4	25 USD	0.985%	30 USD	0.742%	28 USD	2.643%	39 USD
Total CLV	500 USD		555 USD		531 USD		633 USD
CLV INDEX	100%		111%		106%		127%
Price Index	100%		120%		112%		157%

Figure 67: Same scenario as above, but now with quarterly increases instead of annual. Across the lifetime of the customer, this lifts overall cash flow and revenue by half a year's average price increase.

SAAS HYDRAS AND MONOLITHS

The core problem isn't keeping up with inflation but rather how to keep monetizing your own product roadmap over time. There are two immediate, intuitive solutions to that problem: spin out new products to sell, or keep new functionality in your core product and raise prices. Each can fail in its own spectacular way. I call the first approach hydra products and the second monoliths.

A hydra product is one that grows in complexity because every new functionality is introduced as a new module or add-on purchase—even when that makes no technical or commercial sense. Do you remember the Hydra from Greek mythology? It grew two new heads every time one was chopped off. That's what we're dealing with here.

In the myth, the Hydra died at the hands of Hercules. In the real world, hydra products die from increased costs. If you spin out—hydra style—you have to spend CAC you wouldn't otherwise have had to spend, convincing existing customers to buy functionality you would have otherwise simply included in their existing packaging and monetized by raising prices.

Also, the number of different product configurations that sit in your customer base increases exponentially with each new add-on or module release (just five new add-ons create thirty-two different configurations), making it exponentially harder to service those clients. This increases your cost to serve.

Finally, the technical complexity of your product increases with each new add-on, especially as those add-ons are not being created for functional or technical reasons but for a commercial reason: we don't know how else to monetize the product. That makes feedback from users much noisier, thus making product development even more difficult. Also, when there are many more moving parts inside your product, technical development becomes harder as software specs grow and quality assurance time increases. Hence, the cost to develop goes up.

So by spinning out functionality into an add-on, you do get to monetize it. But all your core cost components go up: customer acquisition costs, cost to serve, and cost to develop.

You see hydra products everywhere as "legacy tech" in the market. They addressed a short-term monetization problem with a seemingly innocent, straightforward solution: creating an add-on. But, over time, the number of add-ons multiplied too fast for their underlying economies of scale to keep up until they finally got slow, old, and complex.

That's not necessarily a big problem because such companies still sit on a very lucrative customer base they have acquired over time (all dragons have a hoard of gold). At least, that is, until new, nimble, and unencumbered software solutions come along backed by a never-ending stream of VC capital to try and take their customers away from them. At that time, they are too slow, and their cost base is too heavy; they end up going under. Disruption and innovation 101.

If you're not going down the hydra route, the second obvious solution involves building a monolith (i.e., continually adding functionality to your core product).

In contrast to hydras, monolith products die from under-monetization. If you keep adding functionality without diversifying your core product's packaging or raising prices, you will—assuming inflation—be delivering more and more value for less and less money. List prices might go up for new customers, but old customers stay at their original "legacy" pricing, under-monetized.

Oh, and your costs are likely to go up too. CAC goes up as Sales have a harder time explaining your product to new prospects. There is no packaging to directly and discretely target their jobs to be done, so Sales has to spend time understanding each customer's needs in order to explain to that particular customer how the monolith product can be used to solve their job.

As the customer is unlikely to find uses for *all* the functionality in the monolith product, they are justified in feeling that they are paying for functionality they don't want or need—unless they get a discount. And the larger the monolith, the less of it customers need to solve whatever job they are paying for it to do, so the larger the discounts they will want (and the longer the sales process). That's why even new customers do not pay the increased list prices for a monolith product.

Perversely, the distance between Sales and Product grows with monolith products because it becomes less and less clear what the SaaS business is trying to achieve for customers. Product usually has a unified, holistic, all-in use case in mind. They have a prescriptive mindset. If only customers went all-in on the monolith product, oh, the value that could be created!

But few or no customers actually fit into this monolith vision, which makes it practically unsellable. So Sales, being the practical types they are, are metaphorically stripping the monolith product for parts in the field, trying to sell bits and pieces to customers. Meanwhile, Product is arguing from the comfort of its ivory tower that Sales ought to sell the vision wholesale with no discounts.

As a consequence, CAC increases, development resources are not spent on things that actually create value for customers, and Sales are defensively selling pieces of the monolith at a steep discount instead of offensively focusing on the distinct and valuable jobs that their customers actually have.

OWN YOUR PRICING

So how do you avoid the hydra and monolith pitfalls and still manage to raise prices in step with the increasing value of your product?

First, you have to keep your packaging integrity at all times as you develop your product. Every package should be directed at a particular job that the customer has to do. When your new functionality solves a distinct new job for your customer, you should create a new offering around it. That is how you avoid becoming a monolith. But if your new functionality simply helps solve one of your existing jobs so it can be done better, it should be added to whatever offering you've already built around that job. That way, you don't become a Hydra.

Then, second, you should reassess price points often and change them accordingly, which in most cases means raising them. The necessary foundation for this is that you agree right from the get-go, in the original negotiations and contract you have with your customer, that you can change prices without triggering a renegotiation.

Let's take a look at that in more detail.

CONTRACT FRAMEWORK: DYNAMIC PRICES FROM THE GET-GO

Your SaaS contract should:

1. Give you a perpetually recurring legal and commercial relationship with the customer (i.e., no fixed end date).

2. Enable you to change prices and discounts, products, and operational terms and conditions without renegotiating the contract.

3. Be the same for all customers to allow bulk handling and changes.

This should be easy for every B2C SaaS business out there. Consumers know that prices, product packages, and even terms and conditions can change at the drop of a hat. At the same time, the volume of customers is bigger, allowing for easier price testing. So B2C SaaS businesses are, by and large, better at capturing product value by continually updating their offering and pricing.

When it comes to B2B, though, it's a different story. I see a lot of B2B SaaS contracts that look something like this: "[Customer] is buying [product] from [SaaS business] at [$$ per year], paid annually. The contract lasts for three years after which it can be extended as per mutual acceptance."

The actual contract itself is often a Word template that is being sent around between sales reps, copy-pasted, amended, and flavored by adding each rep's favorite terms and conditions (I wish I was kidding). So each customer gets something unique because there is no stable contract framework in place.

Why is this bad? If customers are buying and contracts are long term at good money, why not? The simple answer is that your future will be a lot less bright and a heck of a lot more troublesome.

If the contract isn't perpetually recurring, you will have to renegotiate it on a recurring basis, which means recurring sales costs. And with each renegotiation, the customer is likely to squeeze you—either for discounts, specialized product configurations, bespoke development, or changes in terms and conditions, all of which are bad things.

If you can't change prices, discounts, and product delivery without triggering a renegotiation, you end up in the hydra and monolith scenarios previously described. If you can't change terms and conditions like payment intervals, cancellation periods, the scheduling of annual status meetings, the assignment of an account manager, and the intervals at which reporting is given—all the tiny, non-core, *operational* details that get lodged inside contracts—you get stuck with a specific operational setup that you can't change, even if you and your customer both agree that there is a better way. And yes, I put payment intervals and cancellation periods in there too as they are mostly an operational function once the relationship is stable.

Finally, if your contract framework is unstable, and you end up with twenty different contracts for twenty different customers, it becomes operationally impossible to go back and change anything. This has a snowball effect as you grow.

Imagine if you closed your first $1M ARR on twenty crazy contracts; you now have a semi-serious problem. These customers might be under-monetized. They might require special handling to renegotiate, upsell, etc. But fixing these issues is hard and takes time and resources from your sales reps (who might also be emotionally tied to some of these "great deals"). And you need to grow another 40 percent this quarter.

So you leave those tricky problems unsolved and close the next $1M ARR on twenty *new*, wildly different contracts. By $5M ARR, this is now a serious problem. By $10M ARR, your legacy customers are now taking up a huge portion of your time and attention. You are constantly renegotiating with a bunch of them. And if one of your senior sales reps leaves, nobody really knows what deal was struck with his major customers.

The lack of flexibility in the network of legal agreements you have with your customers is actually a large contributing factor slowly pushing you into becoming a hydra or a monolith. That's simply because dealing with your contract issues once and for all seems like commercial suicide. It's easier to just keep doing what you've been doing while promising to "do better" with the next contracts you sign.

There is a better way.

THE DYNAMIC SAAS CONTRACT FRAMEWORK

Here is the paraphrased version of a good B2B SaaS contract:

1. [Customer] is a customer of [SaaS business] until [Customer] chooses to cancel this contract as per [cancellation terms].

2. This contract is governed by [general terms, definitions, legislation, etc.].

3. The [Customer]'s purchases at any time are given in [Appendix 1—Overview of Selected Purchases], which will be replaced in full if purchases are updated.

4. Prices and payment terms are listed in [Appendix 2—Catalog of Products and Services] and are subject to change.

5. For an overview of the current setup of our joint operational relationship, please refer to [Appendix 3—Playbook], which is subject to change.

And if you really need to, you can add:

6. It is further agreed that [Appendix 2 or 3] will not change for [insert number of years].

7. It is further agreed that a discount is granted for [limited duration], [discount mechanism], and [amount] as pertaining to [specific product purchase].

There are two key features of this setup. First, your prices and product descriptions actually sit outside of the framework itself, together with the operational features, in appendices that are subject to change whenever you decide they should change. The only thing that sits inside the framework is the—in itself, empty—fact that the customer is a customer and a description of the conditions that relate to that relationship. (I usually say that the contract should "secure the customer, not the purchase.")

The second key feature follows from the first: precisely because the content of the purchase is subject to change at your discretion, this contract framework never triggers a renegotiation, which puts you in a vastly better position. Sure, you can negotiate about new purchases but not about what has already been bought. So you can make all necessary changes to your product and your commercial setup without the specific consent of your customer. Instead, their consent is implicit because of their continued business with you. Technically, you've placed your customer in a negotiation situation where they have to accept your changes as an ultimatum. If they don't like them, they can leave.

It is precisely because this is a long-term, recurring contract that you want to optimize your long-term negotiating position in it—at scale, across all your customers. If you add +20 percent value to your solution every year and manage to redesign your packaging to better allow for targeting of specific customer jobs while also getting smarter about how to handle basic operational issues in the customer relationship, this framework will allow you to smoothly transition to that increased monetization.

To maintain integrity and standardization across contracts, you should ensure that a large block of the contract is simply never negotiated and never can be negotiated. Those blocks are all the grey boxes in Figure 68, which shows what a dynamic B2B SaaS contract should look like.

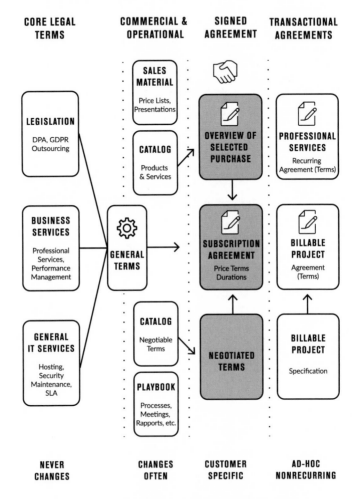

Figure 68: Layout of a SaaS contract framework I've used to create recurring revenue contracts that don't overcommit the vendor and allow ongoing changes in pricing and packaging without triggering formal renegotiations.

The aspects of the contract that are negotiable (i.e., the catalog of what is for sale and some specific terms) should be determined by Sales management, not sales reps. Then, using the list provided by Sales management, the sales reps can determine what is bought and at what negotiated terms, such as discounts and lock-in of the product and price catalog for a period of time (see points six and seven in the features of a good contract, in the previous graphic).

If the customer wants transactional purchases, like an implementation project or some other one-off, that should be put in a separate contract, which can be added to the core subscription contract as an appendix, if necessary.

SELLING THE CONTRACT FRAMEWORK

The one drawback to dynamic contract frameworks is that procurement departments in large corporations don't like them. They like very predictable contracts with lots of leverage to get out and lots of opportunities to press prices and terms at a later stage.

You have to insist on the obvious here: your product is a living thing that will keep evolving to better and better create value for the customer. Because you invest continuously in the product, it will change—radically—over time. That means whatever the customer is signing on to buy today is not going to be what you are delivering in a few years' time. This is actually one of the core selling points of SaaS: the solution is not fixed in time and can develop as the software vendor acquires a deeper and deeper understanding of their customers' jobs to be done.

The core *quid pro quo* of a dynamic contract is that you don't try to tie the customer in for multiple-year contracts. In fact, I often advise my clients to create asymmetrical cancellation clauses that allow the customer to leave within one or a few months while we—the vendor—cannot cancel a contract with less than twelve to twenty-four months' notice. For very large ACVs and public customers with annual budget cycles, it can make sense to extend cancellation terms to one year but never go above this.

A static contract framework that tries to pretend you can agree today on what the right commercial relationship is going to be tomorrow is setting that relationship up for failure. Not only does the dynamic contract actually match the underlying nature of a relationship built upon an evolving product, but it can also give customers all the predictability they want through discounts and "grace periods" where pricing and terms are fixed. They just can't get it in perpetuity.

Salesforce famously offered 90 percent discounts on the first year of their subscriptions, followed by 80 percent the following year, all the way down to a zero percent discount after ten years. By which point, whoever made the decision to buy was probably long gone.

If you have to focus on just one thing to improve your contract, this is it: Can you raise prices without triggering a formal renegotiation? If yes, you're better than 80 percent of B2B SaaS contracts out there.

CASE STORY—ITERAS

Iteras is a Danish B2B SaaS company that delivers a subscription-management solution to magazines and newspapers. I was helping them negotiate a large contract with a potential customer who had more than two million subscribers and had decided to migrate from its existing legacy subscription-management platform because it didn't have the necessary functionality.

Iteras was asking the customer to sign another five-year contract, but when the customer was asked to accept that the pricing and product would change annually, they naturally didn't like it. They wanted to know exactly what they were buying at exactly what price. They even said, "We were with our last vendor for twelve years and imagine we would be with our new vendor for a similar time," implying that their business would be very valuable to Iteras.

I then pointed out, "We don't want you for only twelve years. We want to be a permanent part of your business because you keep choosing us as your partner. If you insist on fixing your purchase and pricing now, instead of trusting that we will develop with you, you will force us to spin out every new innovation as a paid add-on or module, just like the vendor you are leaving did. And you will be tired of us already in five years' time, just like you have been tired of your existing vendor for the past seven years."

They signed.

CONTRACT COHORTS AND PRICING CYCLES

There are two ways to raise prices for a SaaS business: you can raise prices for new customers only, or you can raise prices for both new and old customers.

There are pros and cons to each. Raising prices for all customers simultaneously is operationally easier as you only have to run one line of communication to everyone. You also increase your ARR faster to the new price level, which means money in the bank quicker. On the downside, the risk of churn and serious customer satisfaction issues are considerable across your entire customer portfolio on your new pricing.

Instead, what often happens—and this is especially common for medium to large ACVs—is the following: you test your pricing on new customers, and only once this pricing is proven to work in the market do you go back to your existing customers and increase prices for them. The argument that "this is what your competitor has been paying for six months" is strong when convincing someone that a price is fair and market appropriate.

If you are a high-growth company and want to maximize the monetization potential of your product, you can end up raising prices quite a few times. Quarterly is not unheard of. In fact, it's probably recommended. If you are growing +300 percent a year, the vast majority of your customers at any point in time will have been with you less than a year anyway. This means that none of them will have been around long enough to really be upset with all the price increases. Yet.

Still, some will have been around since the beginning, and even though the early customers might not be that significant from a revenue perspective, you might still have deep collaborations with them, have taken them on stage at trade shows, written customer cases around them, etc. Because of this, maybe you don't want to raise prices for *all* your customers all the time—enter the concept of "pricing cohorts."

A pricing cohort is simply any group of customers that is closed on a specific pricing and product scheme. If your pricing or packaging changes, any customers closed on this new model are now in a new cohort.

So you have two time lines that you work with: when a customer is closed and what pricing and product framework they currently sit under.

PRICING COHORTS

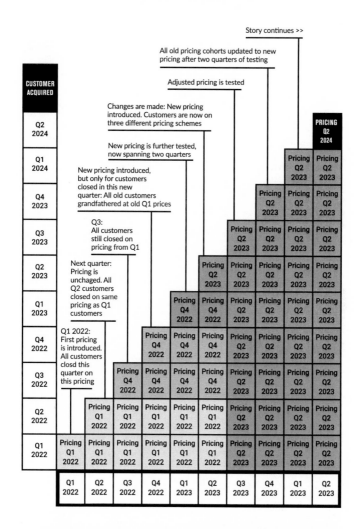

TIMELINE: WHICH COHORT HAD WHAT PRICING WHEN?

Figure 69: Pricing cohorts allow you to keep track of which customers are closed at what prices. This is a key aspect of reducing "commercial debt"—the complexity and operational drag that arises from supporting a hodgepodge of different commercial agreements without a clear system.

The vertical column in Figure 69 shows the quarter in which the customer was acquired (e.g., Q1 of 2022). On the horizontal column, you see a time line going forward. Each row in the cohort overview represents one cohort; the bottom row represents the full time line of pricing for the customers closed in Q1 of 2022, where we can see that they remained at the "Pricing Q1 of 2022" until Q4 of 2023 when they changed to "Pricing Q2 of 2023."

The scenario here is that the SaaS company has pricing in place. Then in Q4 of 2022, they test new pricing but only for new customers signing up in that quarter. Two quarters later—in Q2 of 2023—they change pricing again, maybe because they could see their latest price change wasn't aggressive enough or maybe because their new product roadmap arrived. Then they tested this for two quarters—Q2 and Q3 of 2023—before deciding to update all their customers to this new pricing in Q4 of 2023—a "rollback."

The pricing cohort overview makes it easy to see which customers have had which pricing at what point in time—something that can be surprisingly hard to keep track of. To run it properly, you need to be firm in your shifts from one pricing scheme to the next (e.g., deciding that any leads that receive a demo after April 1 are in the new pricing cohort and then sticking to that).

The first time you do this, expect some operational noise in terms of CRM systems, online pricing pages, etc., but the reward is a unified commercial cadence to run everything in your SaaS organization. You can release new functionality, new packaging, new pricing, etc. in a continuous roll while relatively easily managing who needs to be updated to new price levels and who should be grandfathered for now.

And, full disclosure, what often happens is that 90–95 percent of all customers run in the pricing cohort scheme, while a select few—the very largest of your customers—are simply handled "on the side." They, essentially, are each their own cohort.

Be practical about this. Don't be afraid to take customers that were large and important to you in the past and recognize that if you closed them today, you wouldn't really notice, and then roll them into one of the existing pricing schemes.

COMMUNICATING PRICE CHANGES

People make way too big a deal out of communicating price changes. If you have done your homework and have a good, dynamic contract framework in place, governing a well-packaged product that addresses real customer jobs, and have a nice pricing cohort overview of who has had what prices at what times, then writing the right pricing cohorts with the new pricing is a lot easier than you'd imagine.

The email goes something like this:

Dear XXX,

Prices of your [insert subscription] will change to [new price] per [date].

We continue to develop the best possible product to [do the job they're purchasing the product to do].

Last [month, quarter, year] we released [feature] and [feature] and next [month, quarter, year] we are releasing [feature] and [feature].

Best regards,

That's it. It should not take more than ten minutes to write.

If you have very large ACVs above $100K, you might want to break the news to them in a meeting. That is fine, as long as you are crystal clear that this is not an invitation to a negotiation but rather a friendly FYI and an opportunity you give them to ask questions and feel appreciated.

Yet, if you absolutely must have some "airbags" and risk-reduction mechanisms in your pricing updates, here are a couple of my favorite tools: staged rollbacks across revenue quartiles and time-limited grandfathering.

STAGED ROLLBACKS ACROSS REVENUE QUARTILES

It can be beneficial to stage the rollback of new pricing to your existing customers over a set period—say 25 percent of customers every Monday for four weeks.

This allows you to pump the brake if you made a mistake and only take the hit of one-quarter of your customers screaming bloody murder at you. Also, if there are some operational customer-service tasks involved, you get to spread them out over a longer period of time.

If you want a slightly more sophisticated version of this, divide your current customers into four equal portions of ARR instead, which I call a "revenue quartile." If you rank your customers from large to small, you'll find that you probably have some form of an 80/20 distribution going on where a small portion of your customers makes up a disproportionately large part of your total ARR.

Rolling over one quartile at a time to the new pricing evens out the ARR at risk in each roll and also allows you to make appropriate adjustments in terms of communication and method. For example, maybe you want to have in-person meetings with the five large customers you have that make up 25 percent of your ARR while you are happy simply sending an email to the 5,000 smaller ones that make up the "bottom" 25 percent.

TIME-LIMITED GRANDFATHERING

If you are afraid of churn when rolling out new pricing, you can create a time-limited grandfathering period for your existing customers.

Netflix famously did this. They had raised prices from $7.99 to $8.99 in 2016 and had received a surprisingly large backlash on this, with some serious double-digit churn as a result. So when they raised prices again in 2017, from $8.99 to $9.99, they did so only for new customers while telling existing customers that this would not go into effect before January 2018—a full sixteen months out from the communication.

That amounts to a negative call to action. Even if a customer takes offense at the price increase, they have so much time to react and find a new vendor that they don't do anything about it now. Or next month. Or the month after. Until, finally, the date arrives when prices actually do increase, by which point they've sort of implicitly agreed to accept the new pricing.

The trick here is to have a good sense of your customers' time horizons. What is "a long time" for them? One month? Three months? A full year? Two? Don't sweat this; what you are trying to do is find the optimal exchange between forsaking revenue now in terms of immediate price increases compared to the smaller loss due to lower churn if you postpone those increases.

You don't have enough information to predict this with

certainty. Spend ten minutes discussing it within the management team, then pick a time frame, and move on.

A sidenote to time-limited grandfathering—if you are a VC-funded startup, you probably get to raise your next round on "run-rate ARR," meaning the ARR when it has normalized after current signed customers are onboarded, time-limited discounts have run out, etc. This usually also includes price increases that are announced but not yet in effect.

Case in point: I helped Helloproper.com—a rental property management software company—optimize prices from €7 per unit to €15 in 2022. But because the price increase was so large (doubling), the founders were anxious to just announce new pricing to their existing customers, afraid that it might cause undue churn ahead of their next funding round.

So we simply announced price increases to all existing customers by January 1, 2023—a full nine months later—while stressing that every new customer was already paying €15/unit for the service.

The subsequent funding round took the full €15/unit price in as the measurement of their run-rate ARR when calculating their pre-money, because this was already a proven price in the market and existing customers had already been told.

Turns out you *can* have your cake and eat it too.

HOW TO GET IT DONE IN THE SAAS ORGANIZATION

I hope I've managed to expand your view of what pricing is and give you some real concrete insights, frameworks, and examples you can pick up and put to practice in your own SaaS business.

I advise you to take any pricing work in two steps: first, just get started. Use the tools in this book to create packaging and pricing that your customers will love. Validate it and then implement it. It is not going to be perfect, but it has a high likelihood of being the absolute best use of your time for the next three months and totally transforming your business. Just do it.

Second...well, to be honest, 70 percent of my clients never get to *second*. They are happy with doubling growth, solving their net-dollar-retention issue, or suddenly seeing LTV/CAC shoot way past best in class.

But a few want more. They ask questions like, "How do we 'do' pricing on an ongoing basis?" They don't want projects. They want pricing as a core capability. A commercial North Star that ties together Product, Sales, and Customer Success and keeps it tied together.

I tell these clients that pricing in an organizational context really boils down to being able to answer four questions consistently:

1. What should we build next?

2. How should we package that into sellable products?

3. How should we price that?

4. How much should we price that?

I've dubbed these "The Four Questions of Pricing." They are interdependent. What you should build depends on what you ultimately can charge for it. So schedule it into an annual context that fits the cycle and tempo of your organization.

If you run a data model like PricingRoadmap.com, you could do quarterly model updates, with fresh conjoint surveys of new potential features stacked against old ones. You could then model packaging and pricing scenarios to ultimately decide which roadmap features will increase ARR growth the most.

If you don't run a data model—maybe because your ACV is large and each customer solution is bespoke—you could simply do a similar process, but more qualitatively. Have product and sales rank and discuss roadmap features, in the context of actual product packaging and pricing, ultimately deciding on what to build based on the expected commercial outcome. You could then validate potential models with customers before you commit. And maybe you only do this biannually.

The core issue is realizing you will have to answer the four questions regularly and with a repeatable process that the rest of the organization can get used to over time.

Consider who owns each of the four questions, what process they use to answer, and what tools and resources they need to do so, and you're off to a good start. Then get those people in a room on a regular basis to make actual decisions. You can wrap it up nicely in your org chart, but that—in a nutshell—is your Pricing Function.

It's not easy. Pricing crosses over and touches the domains of almost all the individual functions in the SaaS organization. It "butts in" and interrupts. It demands cohesion and integration across the organization. You can't create that pricing model with this sales setup. Those new features really don't fit the Job-to-Be-Done.

But that's what makes Pricing so powerful: it isn't about you. It's not even about your product. When we talk about Product, Sales, Customer Success, and pricing models, it's all lined up toward creating one, unified North Star for your entire organization: your customer. Price your customer.

EXECUTIVE SUMMARY

Now that you've read the whole book, here's a handy executive summary of the key points. I hope you find it helpful.

CHAPTER 1: WHY PRICING IS HARD

- Pricing is hard because you are trying to price your SaaS product.

- Don't. Instead, price your customer.

- Pricing your customer means price discrimination, so different customers pay different amounts.

- You do that by using two tools: product packaging and pricing models.

- Think trains: first, second, and third class. And the longer you go, the more you pay.

- If you get the product structure and pricing model right, the price points are less important.

- There is a specific sequence you should follow to get it right, which is what the rest of the book is about.

CHAPTER 2: SCALE ECONOMICS

- Strategy is your plan to get and keep a competitive advantage.

- A competitive advantage means having sustainably superior profits.

- Superior profits come from scale and scale only.

- There are three types of scale: cost, product, and distribution.

- There are three types of scale dynamics: critical mass, diminishing returns, and linear.

- "Winner-takes-all" markets happen only when products block competitors.

- Customer lifetime value (CLTV)/customer acquisition cost (CAC) is the most important ratio.

- Each type of scale affects that ratio differently.

- Use the CUPID model to design scale into your product ecosystem.

- Build strategy to achieve scale; use your pricing strategy to support your business strategy.

CHAPTER 3: PRODUCT MODEL

- Your product model covers everything you sell and who you sell it to.

- It has two levels: product ecosystem and packaging.

- The two design principles for creating a product model are fencing and laddering.

- Fencing is separating customers into different overall product and pricing categories.

- Good fences must be discreet, stable, fair, obvious, and valuable.

- Laddering is the structure that determines what customers within each fence pay.

- Every step on the ladder should clearly address a job that the customer has to get done.

- Packaging based around customers' jobs to be done is easier to price and sell.

- It is important to recognize that a problem is not necessarily a job.

- The product ladder should tell a compelling story to encourage customers to ascend it.

CHAPTER 4: PRICING MODEL

- Contrary to popular belief, pricing models should not be simple.

- They should be easy to sell, but that is not the same as being simple.

- A pricing model determines what your customer pays based on what they buy.

- It also structures how that price is different from customer to customer.

- The "complexity toolbox" has three elements, each of which has three sub-elements:

  ◦ Transactional nonrecurring fees, made up of setup fees, ad-hoc one-offs, and exit fees.

  ◦ Flat fees, made up of flat base, flat add-on, and flat non-optional fees.

  ◦ Metric-based fees can be license fees, consumption/usage-based, or credit-based.

- Of the three, metrics are king, making up the majority of your revenue at all annual contract values (ACVs).

- The four key parameters for evaluating a metric are operationally viability, demand, expectation to pay, and metric density.

CHAPTER 5: WALLET STRUCTURING

- Enterprise software is normally bought by a committee ("the Wallet").

- Every member of that committee has their own budget.

- Map your pricing onto that organizational/budget structure to "make everybody pay."

- Your primary buyer should pay because of your product's value.

- The auxiliary buyers should pay because of their expectation to do so.

- Wallet structuring determines what complexity you should add to your pricing architecture.

- Start by listing and categorizing the things you are currently delivering.

- Then, evaluate each budget owner's expectation to pay.

- When setting prices for each item, ensure you don't charge way above *perceived* costs.

- Wallet structuring allows you to price according to value *and* in a cost-plus fashion.

CHAPTER 6: PRICE POINTS

- Prices are not high or low on an absolute basis— only relative to something else.

- When determining a price, people tend to be "anchored" to the first piece of information they get, irrespective of whether it is relevant.

- What prices are relative to is determined by competition and customer sophistication.

- Customer sophistication is driven by frequency, insight, data, and priority.

- It determines the degree of information asymmetry between you and your customer.

- Competitive pricing pressure and customer sophistication can be mapped using the Behavioural Pricing Matrix.

- The four pricing scenarios that make up the matrix are cost-based pricing, niche-based pricing, perceived-value pricing, and fair-value pricing.

- Price points can be determined by internal expert judgment, price experimentation and discovery, customer surveys and interviews, and statistical prediction models.

CHAPTER 7: VALIDATION

- There are four main ways to check that your prices make sense: your judgment, customers' feedback, survey data, and selling in the market.

- It's important to remember that customers want you to have good pricing (i.e., a good method of exchanging value with you).

- When validating, focus on customers who don't buy and listen to "the quality of the no."

- The type of no can help you identify your problem: it could be bad capability, fencing, packaging, or pricing models, or it could be being too expensive or communicating poorly.

- Good pricing has to make sense to your customers. If it doesn't, redesign it.

- There is a simple structure to follow when validating prices through customer interviews.

- Simply structured customer surveys can also be good validation tools when you're in a hurry.

- Market testing is the gold standard of validation; if you're not getting sales, listen to the quality of the no to determine if it is the price or the product that is at fault.

CHAPTER 8: DISCOUNTS

- Discounts tend to be disdained by pricing experts, but they can be a powerful tool.

- The main types are structural and sales discounts (the minor type is post-sales discounts).

- Sales discounts are generally determined on an individual, customer-by-customer basis.

- Structural discounts are predetermined discounts, which are often openly shown in negotiations.

- Such discounts should not be owned by Sales (instead, they should be centralized and owned by either Senior Management or a dedicated Pricing Function).

- Your discount structure should be bigger than your current customers so that they, and any larger customers who come along, can understand where they fit within that structure.

- Sales discounts should only be given reluctantly, to communicate to the customer that they have reached the limit beyond which no further discounting is possible.

- The discount priority order is time limited, short duration; time limited, long duration; terms and conditions; upsell with permanent discount; permanent discount on preferred product.

- Standard operating procedures help to control how your sales reps use discounts.

- Post-sales discounts can prevent churn proactively, reactively, or through grandfathering.

CHAPTER 9: RAISING PRICES

- Price rises should happen frequently—at least annually, if not quarterly.

- Because SaaS products continually develop, you don't know how their value will increase.

- Therefore, avoid contractually fixing future prices to create scope for regular updates.

- Continually adding new modules to your product risks turning you into a Hydra who dies from increased costs.

- Alternatively, continually adding functionality to your core product risks turning you into a monolith that dies from under-monetization (i.e., delivering more value for less money).

- Avoid becoming a Hydra or monolith by keeping your packaging integrity, focusing on customers' jobs to be done, and continually reassessing (and, usually, raising) prices.

- A dynamic-contract framework should give you a perpetually recurring legal and commercial relationship, enabling you to change prices and terms without renegotiating.

- Price rises can either be for all customers or just for new customers; establishing pricing cohorts can help you to manage who is being charged what and when.

- Don't make a big deal out of price changes: keep communication simple.

- Staged rollbacks and time-limited grandfathering can be used to reduce the risk of churn.

GLOSSARY

- **ACV**—annual contract value. The average gross monetary value of one of your customers

- **Ad-hoc one-offs**—all the transactional fees charged during a customer's lifetime

- **Amortization**—the paying off of a balance sheet item in equal installments over time by expensing it on your profit-and-loss account.

- **Anchoring**—the tendency to base any estimate or judgment on the first piece of information received, regardless of whether it is relevant

- **API**—application programming interface

- **ARPA**—average revenue per account

- **ARPU**—average revenue per user

- **ARR**—annual recurring revenue

- **B2B**—business-to-business

- **B2C**—business-to-consumer

- **Bayesian inference modeling**—a process that starts with a baseline assumption and then updates the probability of an event (e.g., whether a lead will result in a sale) based on each new piece of information

- **Behavioural Pricing Matrix**—framework used to map the influence of competitive pricing pressure and customer sophistication on the reference points by which customers evaluate a price point

- **Business strategy**—a company's plan for how to enjoy sustainable, high-profit margins

- **CAC**—customer acquisition cost, usually represented as the average cost to acquire a customer

- **CapEx**—capital expenditure, as opposed to operational expenditure or OpEx

- **Churn rate**—the rate at which a business loses customers over time

- **CIO**—chief information officer

- **CLTV**—customer lifetime value (its components are ARPA, DDC, churn rate, and CAC)

- **Commercial model**—made of a company's acquisition, product, pricing, and service models

- **Complementary product**—a product that can be used alongside another product instead of substituting it

- **Consumption and usage-based metrics**—all metrics that are charged based on behavior where the volume or amount purchased is not determined in advance

- **Cost-based pricing**—prices set as a markup based on underlying costs. Occurs in the Behavioural Pricing Matrix when you are under high, competitive pressure selling to a sophisticated customer

- **Cost scaling**—the improvement of unit economics that occurs when development and delivery costs (DDC) does not increase at the same rate as ARR

- **Credit**—a right to consume or use something at a later stage

- **Credit-based metrics**—a hybrid model between licenses and consumption-based metrics but where the usage is estimated and paid for upfront in return for credits

- **Critical mass scaling**—occurs when the rate of scale is initially low until a tipping point is reached and the rate of scale accelerates with each new unit added

- **CRM**—customer relationship management

- **CSR**—corporate social responsibility

- **CUPID**—Acronym for customers, users, product, iteration, distribution. A framework model to design SaaS product ecosystems and scale

- **Customer sophistication**—a measure of how much information asymmetry exists between a company and a customer, specifically in the context of The Behavioural Pricing Matrix

- **DDC**—development and delivery costs

- **Depreciation**—the decrease in an asset's value over time and the accounting method used to allocate an asset's costs over its life span

- **Diminishing returns**—a scaling dynamic that starts off linear but then drops off at a certain level (like a reverse critical mass)

- **Distribution scaling**—the reduction of CAC for each additional customer acquired, improving overall unit economics

- **ERP**—enterprise resource planning

- **ETP**—expectation to pay (determined by habit, cost transparency, and similarity)

- **Exit fees**—all charges put on a customer as they leave

- **Fair-value pricing**—occurs when a company sells a product under low competitive pressure to a sophisticated customer for a price that distributes the value created from the deal relatively evenly between the seller and the customer

- **Fat-tailed distribution of value**—another cause of low-metric density (see also power-law-distributed value) with many unit instances below the price point
- **Fencing**—the separation of customers into overall different product and pricing categories (cf. laddering)
- **Flat add-on fees**—flat, recurring add-ons that are charged due to some product choice but not tied to a metric
- **Flat-base fees**—the fees that occur as a consequence of a customer's core product choice
- **Flat fees**—charges that do not change or fluctuate depending on a metric (i.e., flat base, flat add-on, and flat non-optional fees)
- **Flat non-optional fees**—recurring flat fees that are added regardless of what a customer chooses to buy and do not fluctuate by any metric
- **FMCG**—fast-moving consumer goods
- **GDPR**—General Data Protection Regulation
- **GMV**—gross merchant value
- **Grandfathering**—the practice of not raising prices for some or all existing customers, even though overall list prices are increasing
- **Hydra**—a product that continually grows in complexity because every new functionality is introduced as a new module or add-on purchase (cf. monolith)
- **Implicit fencing**—a structure in which every potential customer has one (and only one) package they should buy, and the aim is to upsell them to a more expensive package
- **IoT**—internet of things
- **ISAE 3000**—International Standard on Assurance Engagements
- **ISV**—independent software vendors

- **Laddering**—the structure that determines what customers within each fence pay (see fencing)
- **Land and expand**—a business strategy that involves focusing on volume (i.e., getting customers very cheaply and quickly) before focusing on profit (i.e., raising prices)
- **License**—the right to use something; the classic SaaS example being a user license
- **Linear scaling**—when scale happens from the very first unit and then continues forever from there
- **Marketing segmentation**—a component of an acquisition model that involves determining the sales process to apply to customers of different values across various channels, etc.
- **MaxDiff**—maximum difference scaling; a method for rating the relative importance of various features/issues
- **Metric-based fees**—perpetually recurring charges that are dependent on some metric (i.e., metric-based license fees, consumption and usage-based metrics, and credit-based metrics)
- **Metric-based license fees**—charges based on the number of licenses that a user purchases
- **Metric density**—the degree to which value is the same across all units of a given pricing metric
- **Monolith**—the result of continually adding functionality to a core product (cf. Hydra)
- **MRR**—monthly recurring revenue
- **MVP**—minimum viable product, the first version of a product that has enough features to be usable
- **Net revenue**—the revenue that's left after immediate costs are taken out
- **Network effects**—the increase of product value per unit as the number of units goes up

- NGO—nongovernmental organization
- **Niche-based pricing**—occurs when companies base their pricing on serving a particular niche within a large and overcrowded marketplace
- **OEM**—original equipment manufacturer
- **OpEx**—operating expenses (cf. CapEx)
- **Perceived-value pricing**—see value pricing
- **Point of first demand**—the feature of a product/service that has the most articulated and accessible demand stream (i.e., the one that is easiest to sell)
- **Post-sales discounts**—discounts offered to existing customers to prevent churn
- **Power law distributed value**—occurs when most of a metric's value is lodged in a few units, thus creating a low metric density
- **Price Perception Matrix**—measures a product or service's value to a customer alongside their expectation to pay for it
- **Pricing cohort**—any group of customers who is closed on a specific pricing and product scheme
- **Pricing model**—the mechanism that determines what a customer pays based on what they buy
- **Product model**—covers everything a company sells and who it sells it to. Consists of two levels: product ecosystem and packaging
- **Product scaling**—targets increasing product value
- **ROI**—return on investment
- **Run-rate ARR**—the ARR when it has normalized after current signed customers are onboarded, time-limited discounts have run out, etc.
- **SaaS**—software as a service

- **Sales discounts**—determined on a customer-by-customer basis dependent on individual circumstances
- **Scale of distribution**—where CAC decreases based on the number of customers
- **Setup fees**—any fees charged as part of onboarding a customer
- **SLA**—service-level agreement
- **SMB**—small- and medium-sized businesses
- **SOPs**—standard operating procedures; also sales operating procedures
- **Staged rollback**—introducing price changes one set of customers at a time over a set period
- **Strategy**—a company's plan to get and keep a competitive advantage
- **Structural discounts**—predetermined discounts that are often openly shown to customers in negotiations
- **Substitute product**—a type of product where it only makes sense to have one
- **Threshold discounts**—a model in which a discount is universally applied once the customer passes through a certain threshold (cf. waterfall discounts)
- **Transactional-nonrecurring fees**—any charges that aren't perpetual or recurring, made up of setup fees, ad hoc one-offs, and exit fees
- **Users as customers**—the straightforward situation in which users pay to use a product
- **Users as distribution**—the situation in which users act as a distribution channel through which paying customers can be reached
- **Users as product**—the situation in which users are aggregated and sold to a customer (e.g., an advertiser)

- **Value pricing**—determining price based on customers' perceptions of a product's worth and their willingness to pay for it, rather than on production costs (in the context of The Behavioural Pricing Matrix, pricing conditions that occur when no or low competition is present)

- **Van Westendorp**—a four-question survey to determine price sensitivity

- **Wallet**—the committee of buyers at any organization, each of whom normally has their own budget, who decide whether or not to purchase a product/service

- **Wallet structuring**—the designing of a pricing model so that it targets several discreet budgets within your customer's organization

- **Waterfall discounts**—a model in which discounts are only applied to units above a certain volume (i.e., the first units have a higher price than the last units) (cf. threshold discounts)

- **Whale**—one of the largest customers in a market

- **Winner-takes-all market**—occurs when products block their competitors because customers only need one version of the product